HALLOWED BE THY NAME

HALLOWED BE THY NAME

A SPIRITUALITY FOR TODAY

JIM MCMANUS CSsR

DARTON · LONGMAN + TODD

First published in 1996 by
Darton, Longman and Todd Ltd
1 Spencer Court
140 – 142 Wandsworth High Street
London SW18 4JJ

ISBN 0-232-52129-8

A Catalogue record for this book is available
from the British Library

Biblical quotations are taken from the Jerusalem Bible,
published and copyright © 1966, 1967 and 1968 by
Darton, Longman and Todd Ltd and Doubleday & Co Inc.

Phototypset by Intype London Ltd
Printed and bound in Great Britain by
Redwood Books, Trowbridge

To six very special friends
who have always made me feel at home:
my three sisters-in-law and
my three brothers-in-law.

Contents

Introduction

In the past we talked a great deal about knowing the faith, keeping the faith, practising the faith. Today we talk about sharing the faith or, more commonly, faith sharing.

In its original form this book was a training programme in faith sharing. The book began to germinate in 1989. We were about to enter the decade of the nineties, the last decade before the third millennium. Pope John II had called for 'a decade of evangelisation'. Although there are well over a billion Christians in the world there are an increasing number of people who have never heard of Jesus Christ, have no specific faith in God, and who are searching for some meaning in their lives. We Christians have good news for them. But, so often we keep this good news to ourselves. It is as if we understand the injunction 'keep the faith' to mean 'keep the faith to ourselves'!

I often think about the man from whom Jesus cast out the legion of demons. He was obviously very grateful to Jesus for his new found health and wholeness. As a sign of his gratitude he wanted to follow Jesus with the other group of disciples. St Mark writes:

> AS HE WAS GETTING INTO THE BOAT, THE MAN WHO HAD been possessed begged to be allowed to stay with him. Jesus would not let him, 'Go home to your people and tell them all that the Lord in his mercy has done for you'. So the man went off and proceeded to spread throughout the whole Decapolis all that Jesus had done for him. Everyone was amazed. (Mark 5:19-20)

That ex-demoniac knew how to share his faith in Jesus. He simply told people what the Lord had done for himself.

There is a great difference between telling people about Jesus and telling people what Jesus has done for oneself. Sometimes you find people who have a vast knowledge of the faith but who are incapable of telling others what the Lord has done for themselves. Conversely, you can find people who are not too well versed in the faith but who can easily and effectively tell others what the Lord has done for them. It is not a question of knowledge but of freedom from inner inhibitions. Many people have acquired the facility of talking objectively about God 'out there', but remain totally inhibited when they try to talk about God in their own lives. Training in faith sharing has to focus on these inhibitions. We must find a simple, natural way of talking about what God is doing in our own lives.

We tend to use the word 'faith' in two quite distinct ways. Theologians have always distinguished between the **faith which we believe** (*fides quae*) and the **faith by which we believe** (*fides qua*). The **faith which we believe** is expressed in the Bible, in the tradition of the Church, and is formulated in the doctrine of the Church. We can spend our whole life studying the faith which we believe. Theologians and biblical scholars do that. The **faith by which we believe** is the inner conviction or assurance which enables us to believe. Without the gift of faith we cannot believe. In faith sharing our primary intention is to share the faith by which we believe. We share with another person that inner light of faith which enables us to say: 'Yes, Lord I believe that you are the Christ, the Son of the living God'.

To help people grow in this freedom I developed a twelve step faith-sharing programme entitled Hallowed Be Thy Name. Each step is a reflection on a key aspect of our faith, not an abstract, theological reflection but a pastoral and personal reflection. There is, of course, no conflict between these two approaches to the faith. Both are necessary. In this formation programme, however, I developed a method which would focus on experience: how do I experience God and all that God has done for me in my own life? Thousands of men and women have found this very helpful. In this book I follow the same method. That is why, as you read this book, I will be asking you towards the end of each chapter, to pause for a few moments and enter into a new relationship with God, Father, Son and Holy Spirit, in prayer. The spiritual effectiveness of your reading of this book depends on this pause and this moment of prayer. You will read how the Lord has worked in the lives of a great variety of men and women of all ages and walks of life. As you prayerfully read how they share what the Lord has done in their lives you will grow in your freedom to share what the Lord is doing in your own life. In other words, you will be preparing yourself to share your faith with others. By acquiring this freedom to share with others your own experience of God you will grow and mature in your life of faith.

Speaking about 'mature faith', Pope John Paul II says: 'The evangelising activity of the Christian community, first in its own locality, and then elsewhere as part of the Church's universal mission, is the clearest sign of a mature faith.'[1] A practising parish which has not yet become an evangelising parish is still living by an immature faith. Passing on the faith, bringing the Gospel of Jesus to others, is the sign of maturity of faith. This is true not just for parishes but for each individual member of the Church. Your readiness and willingness to share your faith with others, to share your experience of Christ with others, is the clearest sign of your own maturity of faith.

The parish community is called not only to live the life of faith but also to share that life with others. The mission of the parish is to evangelise. Pope John Paul II says: 'People today put more trust in witnesses than in teachers, in experience than in teaching, and in life and action than in theories. The witness of a Christian life is the first and irreplaceable form of mission.'[2] The parish is a faith community. The common bond between the multiplicity of its members is faith in Jesus Christ. The parish lives this faith as a community of brothers and sisters. It is the quality of their Christian life as a community which gives the primary witness to Christ. As Pope John Paul says: 'The first form of witness is the *very life of the missionary, of the Christian family, and of the ecclesial community,* which reveal a new way of living.'[3]

The parish becomes an evangelising community by the witness of its life. Martin Baile experienced 'this new way of living' in St Boniface's parish in Pembroke Pines, Florida: 'what was beginning to come through to me was the real joy and happiness and commitment in that community. The sharing and caring and praying were all as naturally part of their lives as anything else they did. The enthusiasm was infectious and so genuine.' Martin went with Fr Peter Brett and a few other parishioners from the Redemptorist parish in London to study how St Boniface's parish in Florida has become a beacon of evangelisation for parishes all over the world. The pastor of the parish, Fr Michael Eivers, introduced a new pastoral strategy for the renewal of his parish. A big percentage of his parish now meet once a fortnight in small, cell groups of 10 to 15 people. They meet in each others' homes; they listen to the word of God; they share their faith and praise of God; they share a teaching on video from their pastor; they invite anyone who expresses an interest in God or spiritual things to come and share in their small group. They have become evangelists. The parish has experienced great renewal through this powerful cell movement. It has become an evangelising parish. Martin and his companions returned to their parish of St Mary's, Clapham and under the energetic leadership of Fr Brett they introduced this new strategy. The parish is growing as a community. It is also becoming an evangelising parish.

Another group from the parish went to Milan to study a parish which has grown strong through a similar cell movement. Philomena Walron described her experience of that parish in this way:

THE DEEP PRAYERFULNESS AND COMMITMENT TO JESUS OF the parishioners involved in the workshop and the cells crossed the language barrier and we found ourselves immersed in the love of people walking closely with the Lord and giving their lives in joyful service of him and of each other – in a completely matter-of-fact way. Everyone took ministry for granted: for them working for the Lord in any capacity, evangelisation and a life of prayer went with being a Christian.

Philomena is describing the faith of ordinary men and women who have learnt how to share their faith in Christ and joy in being his disciples.

The purpose of parish renewal is to call people to the work of evangelisation. Many 'practising Catholics' can be in effect 'lapsed evangelists'. Maybe they have never taken their call to be evangelists of Christ seriously? A conversion is needed. Not necessarily a moral or religious conversion but a conversion in the whole way in which they see themselves as Christians in the world. Pope John Paul describes this conversion well when he writes:

A RADICAL CONVERSION OF THINKING IS REQUIRED IN ORDER to become missionary, and this holds true both for individuals and entire communities. The Lord is always calling us to come out of ourselves and to share with others the goods we possess, starting with the most precious gift of all – our faith. The effectiveness of the Church's organisations, movements, parishes and apostolic works must be measured in the light of this missionary imperative. Only by becoming missionary will the Christian community be able to overcome its internal divisions and tensions, and rediscover its unity and its strength of faith.[4]

We need *a radical conversion of thinking*. For far too long we have suffered from the malaise of the privatisation of religion. Our society expected us to treat religion as a purely private matter, something that one should not talk about to others. We developed a fear of being accused of 'pushing religion down people's throat'. None of us would like to be accused of 'proselytising'. The image of the evangelist with a foot in the door is not an appealing one. The truth is, of course, that we can share our faith with others without doing any of these things. Respect for the truth others hold in their hearts would keep us from proselytising while courtesy would keep us from ever seeking to put our foot in the door. The Christian evangelist never behaves as the hard-sell salesperson. Nevertheless, fear has kept many of us from sharing our faith with those who are eager to receive.

Because we have not been formed to share our faith we might find it almost impossible to respond to the simple question: who is God in our life? or who is Jesus Christ in our life? Pope John Paul II says: 'Unless the missionary is a contemplative he cannot proclaim Christ in a credible way. He is a witness to the experience of God, and must be able to say with the Apostles: "that which we have looked upon . . . concerning the word of life . . . we proclaim also to you"' (1 John 1:1–3).[5] The aim of this book is to help you become aware of what God is doing in your own life and prepare you to share that experience of God with others.

An essential part of our original programme for faith sharing was a programme for reading the New Testament. During the twelve step programme, which could be twelve weeks, the participants read through the whole of the New Testament. This was a great blessing in their lives. I have retained this aspect of the programme in this book. At the end of each chapter I will provide a table of New Testament reading. If you read a chapter of this book each week and read the chapters of the New Testament which I indicate, you will have read not only the book but also the whole of the New Testament in twelve weeks. You can do this as part of your own spiritual development. But, if possible, it is much more encouraging to do it in a group. In your parish or locality there may be faith-sharing groups, or prayer groups, or Scripture sharing groups. If there is no group in your parish or community for this kind of sharing perhaps you will feel called to start one? The small group, like the living cell of the body, ensures growth and development of one's faith. We need to belong to a community of faith. We cannot live or share our faith in isolation.

The primary purpose of this book is to help people share

their faith in a simple, personal way. When we acquire this freedom we begin to see that we do not have to be theologians in order to be evangelists. The moment I have the freedom to share my faith in Jesus Christ I have become an evangelist. I have good news for others. The witness of our own personal lives is, of course, the first witness which we offer to Christ. But we are also called to speak about Christ to others. The most effective way any of us can speak about Christ to others is to 'tell them all that the Lord in his mercy has done for us'. If this book helps people to do that, even in a small way, I will be well satisfied.

This book could not have been written without the collaboration and encouragement of many people. My confrère Charles Corrigan collaborated with me in drawing up a new approach to parish missions. In these missions we developed the twelve step training programme which was the origin of this book. Another confrère, Geoffry Wilkins shared the first new-type parish mission with me and together we launched the programme Hallowed Be They Name. I acknowledge my gratitude to them. My thanks too to my confrère Beverly Ahearn who has a keen eye for typographical errors. My special thanks to the men and women, wonderful disciples of the Lord, who have shared their testimonies in this book. They have shared with simplicity and faith 'all that the Lord in his mercy has done for them'. They are true evangelists in today's world. So, my gratitude to Jane, Bernarde, Bob, Damian and Cathy, Phyllis, Angela, Margaret, Michelle and the others who remain anonymous.

I

Hallowed be thy Name

The first big word I ever had to get my tongue around was the word 'hallowed'. I was blessed to be born into a Catholic home where the family rosary was a nightly prayer. We all joined in, all twelve of us, from the youngest to the oldest. When I was about four years old I would be saying my decade and shouting out 'Our Father, who art in heaven, hallowed be thy name.' I never asked myself, of course, what this word 'hallowed' meant. I had learned the prayer by heart and for years I never thought about the meaning of the words. In fact, throughout my whole life as a priest I do not remember anyone ever asking the meaning of the word.

I learned at an early age that God's name is holy and that we should never take his name in vain. The second command-ment, which every child learned at school, states 'You shall not take the name of the Lord your God in vain.' Observing this commandment was a serious duty. God's name is a holy name. We must always use it with reverence. In fact, the most common sin I learned to confess as a boy was 'taking the Lord's name in vain'. Examples of this sin would be saying 'by God I will' or 'by Christ I will'. Indeed, Catholics have an amazing fluency in introducing the holy name of God or Jesus into quite unholy situations. It is not uncommon to hear Catholics use 'Jesus Christ' not as a term of reverence but as an expletive. One of my Redemptorist confrères from Ireland greatly amused a gathering of Redemptorists from Europe by regularly beginning his conversational responses with the words 'arrah Jasus'.

We could discuss at length whether this colloquial abuse of the holy Name is the same thing as 'taking the name of the Lord in vain'. For most people it would seem to be an unconscious, linguistic reflex and it would be rather legalistic to describe this manner of speech in terms of sinning against the second commandment. For any sin we have to act with full knowledge, freedom, and consent. Unconscious habits do not fall within that degree of human awareness. Nevertheless, we should not absolve ourselves too readily from a habit which always results in an abuse of the holy name. There is always something we can do about our unconscious habits.

We are not concerned here, however, with the abuse of the holy name which is such a common occurrence in many Catholic cultures. We are concerned with 'hallowing' God's name. When we pray 'hallowed be thy name' what exactly are we talking about? Are we asking that we hallow God's name by refraining from any behavioural abuse, living in a way which is contrary to God's holiness? Are we asking that God himself hallows his name by coming to save us from our sins?

Since God is all holy and his name is holy how could we make his name holy? How could we hallow his name? The more we think about this the more clearly we will see that we cannot hallow God's name. Although we can abuse his name, 'take it in vain', we ourselves cannot hallow it or make it holy. God alone can make his own name holy. Gerard Lohfink's comments were a great enlightenment to me. He asks:

WHAT IS REALLY MEANT BY THE PRAYER, NOW SO STRANGE to us, that God sanctify his name? Once again the answer is given in the Old Testament, in Ezekiel 36. There it is said that the name of God has been desecrated by the dispersal of Israel among the nations. As a result of this, all the nations say: 'So this is the people of God! This Yahweh must be a miserable God, if he is unable to preserve his own people from the loss of their land!' (cf. Ezek. 36:20). In this situation God speaks through Ezekiel: He says 'But I have been concerned about my holy name, which the House of Israel has profaned among the nations where they have gone. And so, say to the House of Israel, "The Lord Yahweh says this: I am not doing this for your sake, House of Israel, but for the sake of my holy name, which you have profaned among the nations where you have gone. I mean to display the holiness of my great name, which has been profaned among the nations, which you have profaned among them. And the nations will learn that I am Yahweh – it is the Lord Yahweh who speaks – when I display my holiness for your sake before their eyes. Then I am going to take you from among the nations and gather you together from all the foreign countries, and bring you home to your own land" ' (Ezek. 36:23–25). The text clearly shows that *God himself* will sanctify his name.[1]

Notice that it is God himself who is going to display the holiness of his name. His name will be 'hallowed' or 'sanctified' when he saves and delivers his people from their exile and dispersal among the nations of the world. He will bring them 'home to their own land'. He will restore them not just to the land of the promise but he will fulfil in them the promise which he made to their ancestors: he will be their God and they will be his people.

This is, in effect, the promise of salvation – salvation for the people of Israel, our salvation. As God displays the holiness of his name, as he 'hallows' his name, we are sanctified.

The promise of vv. 24–9 is packed full of action verbs and images:

- I am going to take you ... and gather you together.
- I shall pour clean water over you.
- I will cleanse you.
- I will give you a new heart.
- I will put a new spirit in you.
- I shall remove the heart of stone ... and give you a heart of flesh.
- I shall put my spirit in you.
- You shall be my people and I will be your God.

Each one of those great promises contains in itself the whole work of our salvation. 'Hallowed be thy name' is the proclamation of the whole divine enterprise of salvation. When we say 'hallowed be thy name' we are saying pour clean water over us, give us a new heart, put your spirit in us. It is clearly God himself who hallows God's name.

God displays the holiness of his name by doing a great work in us, by making us holy. This was how the early Church understood this prayer. The great African father of the Church, Tertullian, writing in the third century said:

> WHEN WE SAY 'HALLOWED BE THY NAME', WE ASK THAT IT should be hallowed in us, who are in him; but also in others whom God's grace still awaits, that we may obey the precept that obliges us to pray for everyone, even our enemies. That is why we do not say expressly hallowed be thy name 'in us', for we ask that it be so in all men.[2]

When we pray 'hallowed by thy name' we are saying 'save thy people, Lord'.

St Cyprian, writing around the year AD 250 said:

> BY WHOM IS GOD HALLOWED, SINCE HE IS THE ONE WHO hallows? But since he said, 'You shall be holy to me; for I the Lord am holy', we seek and ask that we who were sanctified in Baptism may persevere in what we have begun to be. And we ask this daily, for we need sanctification daily, so that we who fail daily may cleanse away our sins by being sanctified continually ... We pray that this sanctification may remain in us.[3]

Another great Father of the Church St Peter Chrysologus wrote:

> WE ASK GOD TO HALLOW HIS NAME, WHICH BY ITS OWN holiness saves and makes holy all creation ... It is this name that gives salvation to a lost world. But we ask that this name of God should be hallowed in us and through our actions. For God's name is blessed when we live well, but is blasphemed among the Gentiles when we live wickedly. As the Apostle says: 'The name of the God is blasphemed among the Gentiles because of you'. We ask then that, just

as the name of God is holy, so we may obtain his holiness in our souls.[4]

When we say 'hallowed by thy name' we are really saying 'sanctify us, Lord'. The *Catechism of the Catholic Church* expresses the same truth for our time in this way:

AND SO, IN ADORATION, THIS INVOCATION [HALLOWED BE Thy Name] is sometimes understood as praise and thanksgiving. But this petition is here taught to us by Jesus as an optative: a petition, a desire and an expectation in which God and man are involved. Beginning with this first petition to our Father, we are immersed in the innermost mystery of his Godhead and the drama of the salvation of our humanity. Asking the Father that his name be made holy draws us into his plan of loving kindness for the fullness of time, 'according to his purpose which he set forth in Christ' that we might 'be holy and blameless before him in love'.[5]

When we say 'hallowed be thy name' we are really saying 'fulfil the plan you made for us in Christ'. It is in Christ that God's name is totally hallowed. As Carroll Stuhlmueller writes: 'God manifests his holiness and sanctifies his name in Jesus (Mark 1:23; John 12:22) especially at the moment of his return to the Father and his sending of the Spirit (John 16:14).[6]

'Hallowed be thy name' sums up everything that Jesus wants the Father to do in us. Jesus wants the Father to save us, to sanctify us, to protect us from all evil.

When you are worried about your family, or your loved ones, you could not say a better prayer than 'hallowed be thy name'. It contains every good thing that you could possibly wish for them. This is a simple way to pray about any problem: you think of the problem, you offer the problem to God and you say 'Father, hallowed be thy name'. St Alphonsus Liguori, a great Doctor of prayer, encouraged people to share with God 'all their thoughts of fear or of sadness' in an intimate and personal way. Then leave all with God. We do not have to tell God what to do about the problem. In asking God to hallow his name we are asking him to save, sanctify, protect and deliver. Pope John Paul II writes: 'To save means to embrace and lift up with redemptive love, with love that is always greater than any sin.'[7] When we pray 'hallowed be thy name' over our problems we are asking God to embrace and lift us up in his redemptive love.

Jane (not her real name) writes about how she experienced God hallowing his name in her own life. She gave this title to her testimony: 'Abortion – the Journey of Recovery.'

BEFORE I TRAVEL TO THE RENEWAL CENTRE I MUST BEGIN with how indebted I am to Fr P, whom I met last January. He met an angry, foul mouthed, depressed woman – to the point that I felt suicidal, dead and empty within. I had nothing to live for. I had folded up my job. My relationship with a married man had ceased, and I was very much alone with myself. Fr P met me with great understanding, but his words spoken to me on that first meeting really challenged me. He said 'you can't run away anymore, you owe it to yourself. Give yourself time.'

I had been running from myself for 47 years and I hated the mess I was in. He was so right but I hated what I heard. I know it meant I had to unload a huge story, a story too big for me, a story wrapped in fear and guilt and somehow sealed with silence. I think it took two or three meetings with Fr P – meetings which involved a lot of pain, foul language and tears before his gentle approach helped me to trust him with the reason for my pain. My pain was caused mainly by an abortion I had almost three years previously, when I was three months pregnant. His non-judgemental approach to my story and his pastoral care for me, set me on the road to recovery.

He didn't reduce the seriousness of the mess I was in, or offer an instant solution or relief. He knew I had a long healing journey to make, so he encouraged me to take time out and for a period of spiritual renewal. By this time I was in better shape and I had started to trust Fr P. However, the breaking of silence had made me feel very painful, raw and sore within. I was anxious about embarking on a period of spiritual renewal and I went on the course with my mind made up to return to silence, until I met Fr P again.

In the beautiful, quiet peaceful surroundings of the renewal centre I couldn't escape from myself. I coped nicely until Michael arrived and started on Human Development. I agonised for a few days and then decided it was safe to speak with this guy, as he was just passing through. I mustered up the courage to knock on his door one afternoon. I found a very human, caring, understanding person. His concern for my pain was so great that he made arrangements, with Denis, to meet me and journey with me. Once again I was met with understanding and great compassion.

I was struggling with his (God's) interest in an unlovable creature like me. I experienced a very gentle hand of God at work despite the fact that I had locked Him out of my life for a number of years. I had locked myself up in fear, shame and guilt. I had divorced God for another relationship which did not work. It was very painful and humbling to discover that the God whom I had moved away from still loved and cared for me. It was fierce struggling, and tremendous pain to raise one's head bent in shame and meet the eyes of forgiveness and love. God forgave me long before I was able to forgive myself. I was trapped in a cloud of confusion and like Job, I cursed the day I was born, and the day I revealed my story.

They say every cloud has a silver lining. This became real for me on week eight of the course, when Jim arrived. Julian, whom I found to be very gentle, kind and supportive gave me every encouragement to talk with Jim. By this time I was at an all time low, and was pushing myself, just to be physically present in the conference room. By mid-week rumour had it that Jim would be asking us to pray with each other in our small groups, on Thursday morning. Sure enough after the coffee break on the Thursday morning, Jim sent us off into our small groups to experience God at work through our prayerful ministry with each other. I was finding the group work rough going, so I decided I would chat with Jim instead. I waited to catch him while others moved to their groups. On standing there it was as if a little voice said to me 'do what you have been asked to do and leave the rest to me'.

Very, very reluctantly I joined my group. I remember I asked the group to pray with me that I might be able to accept God's love and have the grace to forgive myself. It was a tearful and tremendous healing moment for me. I was able to allow the wall of resistance to crumble. In the love and care of the group for me I discovered people were really carrying my pain in prayer.

This experience greatly strengthened me and enabled me to move on, and face the question Fr P had raised with me some months earlier. He raised the question of the child and how I felt about naming it. At that moment it was, as if a dagger went through my heart. I had had an abortion and to be asked to change this word to child was a huge thing for me. In the weeks and months that followed I had to struggle with words like death and murder. For me I actually experienced this death within myself. I remember saying to Fr P at one stage 'I am so dead and empty that I feel like an empty tin can moving around'.

The moment I was being prepared for happened that afternoon of 23 June 1994. I went out for a stroll in the garden in order to reflect on my morning experience and I met Jim. I stood in front of him and said 'Come with me, I think we have to talk'. I remember I said to him 'I did what you asked me to do with my group, but I feel there is more'. We strolled to one of the garden seats. As I poured out my story to him, I felt Jim turned to me in prayer with great love and concern. After spending some time in prayer he gently approached the question of the child. I was able to accept his suggestions that we name the child during the celebration of the Eucharist. This was a very special celebration for me, a time when I experienced the powerful presence of a healing and forgiving God. In His peaceful presence I named and received baby Pat.

Words alone cannot convey to you the peace and freedom I experienced at that wonderful moment. During the week Jim had been talking about 'Let all that is within you give praise to God'. Inside me were cursing, hate, anger and destruction. I couldn't reconcile what was happening within me to what Jim was asking us to do. However, the next day things were different and I felt a new person, even though I had no sleep. I had spent the night praising God with the words 'let all that is within me cry worthy'. This, for me, was to complete the healing, because in all of it, I would have felt unworthy of what the good Lord was doing for me.

To complete this story I must flash back to an experience I had prior to this time of spiritual renewal. When I would meet with Fr P he would encourage me to spend some time in their prayer room. During one of my visits to the prayer room I had this picture of Mary and the Child in her arms. Mary was presenting me with the child, but I was unable to respond. I remember I withdrew and actually experienced a terrible coldness in my body. I felt I had in some serious way disfigured this image – while on the other hand I had a great sense that Mary was the one who was gently preparing me to receive the child. My first week in the renewal centre a member of the staff greeted a number of us with a beautiful card which had a lovely picture of the Mother and Child on it and the words 'I entrust myself to you, O Mary and rest secure, as a child in its mother's arms'. (Needless to say the card was special for me and I hold it).

That renewal course was for me a time of growth, healing and peace. It holds memories which I will treasure for the rest of my life. I'm eternally grateful to students and staff who encouraged, supported and enabled me to make the journey, a journey into the embrace of God's love and for-giveness and the gift of baby Pat.

This story or testimony is written with joy and gratitude tinged with pain. My prayer and hope is that others may be strengthened and encouraged when they hear or read my story.

In writing her powerful testimony Jane has become an evangelist. She brings good news, gospel, from God. Pope John Paul II said that 'the evangelist is a witness to the experience of God'. Jane has shared with us, with deep faith and utter simplicity, her transforming experience of God. She discovered in her own personal life that it is God himself who hallows his own name and that God displays the holiness of his great name through what he does in us: 'I will pour clean water over you and you will be cleansed ... I will take from your body the heart of stone and give you a heart of flesh ... I will put my own spirit in you.' Jane begins her story with a description of herself 'an angry, foul mouthed, depressed woman – to the point that I felt suicidal, dead and empty within'. She acknowledged the source of her pain: 'My pain was caused mainly by an abortion I had almost three years previously when I was three months pregnant.'

The father of her child was a married man. Her adulterous affair had ended and the baby had been aborted. She was now entirely on her own; she had given up her job; she was thrown back on her own very meagre resources. She confesses: 'I had divorced God for another relationship which did not work.' Her story is so reminiscent of Jesus' own parable of the prodigal son: 'A man had two sons. The younger said to his father, "Father, let me have a share of the estate that would come to me." So the father divided the property between them. A few days later, the younger son got together everything he had and left for a distant country where he squandered his money on a life of debauchery' (Luke 15:11–13). The young prodigal, like Jane, discovered he had very few resources left when the famine came. We read: 'he began to feel the pinch, so he hired himself out to one of the local inhabitants who put him to work on his farm to feed the pigs. And he would willingly have filled his

belly with the husks the pigs were eating but no one offered
him anything.' He is on his own, just as Jane was on her own.
Neither of them have within themselves the resources for their
own salvation. And, salvation begins for both of them when
they decided to make a journey of recovery. The prodigal said:
'I will leave this place and go to my father and say: Father, I
have sinned against heaven and against you; I no longer deserve
to be called your son; treat me as one of your paid servants.
So he left the place and went back to his father.' The prodigal,
like Jane, had a journey to make. Jane described how she felt
on her journey in this way: 'It was very painful and humbling
to discover that the God I had moved away from still loved
and cared for me. It was fierce struggling and tremendous pain
to raise one's head bent in shame and meet the eyes of forgiveness and love. God forgave me long before I was able to
forgive myself'.

The prodigal, on his journey was having the same struggle,
rehearsing his confession and hoping to be accepted as 'one of
your hired servants'. Then he was overwhelmed by the love
and acceptance of the father:

WHILE HE WAS STILL A LONG WAY OFF, HIS FATHER SAW HIM
and was moved with pity. He ran to the boy, clasped him
in his arms and kissed him tenderly. Then his son said,
'Father, I have sinned against heaven and against you. I no
longer deserve to be called your son.' But the father said to
his servants, 'Quick! Bring out the best robe and put it on
him; put a ring on his finger and sandals on his feet. Bring
the calf we have been fattening, and kill it; we are going to
have a feast, a celebration, because this son of mine was
dead and has come back to life; he was lost and is found.'
(Luke 15:20–24)

The prodigal had a celebration. Jane had a night of prayer
and praise with her God. In her pain and isolation Jane had
many fears and doubts. In the loving embrace of the Father all
doubts vanished. She personally experienced the truth of the

words which Pope John Paul II addresses to women who have had an abortion:

> THE CHURCH IS AWARE OF THE MANY FACTORS WHICH MAY have influenced your decision, and she does not doubt that in many cases it was a painful and even shattering decision. The wound in your heart may not yet have healed. Certainly what happened was and remains terribly wrong. But do not give in to discouragement and do not lose hope. Try to understand what happened and face it honestly. If you have not already done so, give yourself over with humility and trust to repentance. The Father of mercies is ready to give you his forgiveness and his peace in the Sacrament of Reconciliation. You will come to understand that nothing is definitively lost and you will also be able to ask forgiveness from your child, who is now living in the Lord.[8]

In Jane's case God's name was hallowed when she accepted 'forgiveness from her child' and gratefully received baby Pat as her son. As she said, 'Words cannot convey the peace and freedom I experienced in that wonderful moment.' Only in the embrace of the Father's love and the forgiveness of the child will the wound in the heart of the mother be healed. In accepting baby Pat, Jane knew the forgiveness of her child. She had returned and she knew she was totally accepted. That divine acceptance empowered her to accept herself as the mother of baby Pat.

Romano Guardini wrote: 'The act of self-acceptance is the root of all things. I must agree to be the person who I am. Agree to have the qualifications which I have. Agree to live within the limitations set for me ... The clarity and the courageousness of this acceptance is the foundation of all existence.'[9] Jane agreed to be the person she was, agreed to be mother of the unborn baby. She realised that she had been trying to build her life on the foundation of a twofold denial: the denial of her motherhood and the denial of the personhood of the unborn baby. Such denial may induce a temporary amnesia but it can never bring peace. The reality of her pregnancy meant that she had become a mother and she had conceived a child. Acceptance, not denial is the only true 'foundation of all existence'. As she accepted her motherhood and named her baby, Jane came into great peace of soul.

God sent different people to minister to Jane on her journey back to self-acceptance and forgiveness. Each of them prepared her for the liberating moment in the Eucharist when she named and accepted her baby and received God's great forgiveness. The celebration of the Eucharist in thanksgiving for the child, and the committal of the child into the loving hands of God heals the trauma of the abortion. Women who have had abortions will find the peace which Jane found when they build the rest of their lives on the foundation of acceptance: acceptance of the reality of motherhood, acceptance of the human reality of the baby who is now with God and acceptance of the loving forgiveness of God when they turn to him with a contrite heart. They will know, too, in Pope John Paul's words 'the forgiveness of your child, who is now living in the Lord'.

Unfortunately so much to do with abortion involves denial – denial of motherhood, denial of the personhood of the aborted baby, denial of the need for forgiveness. Jane, while she was in denial, lived in shame and guilt. Once she accepted the whole reality of her situation and brought it to God she experienced deep inner healing and peace. Pope John Paul II, in his very first encyclical letter to the Church, encourages us to bring all our troubles and sins to Christ. He writes:

THE MAN WHO WISHES TO UNDERSTAND HIMSELF thoroughly – and not just in accordance with the immediate, partial, and often superficial, and even illusory standards and measures of his being – he must with all his unrest, uncertainty and even his weakness and sinfulness, with his life and death, draw near to Christ. He must, so to speak, enter into him with his own self, he must 'appropriate' and assimilate the whole reality of the Incarnation and the Redemption in order to find himself. If this profound process takes place within him, he then bears fruit not only in adoration of God but also of deep wonder at himself.[10]

Jane had that profound experience of 'appropriating and assimilating the whole reality of the Incarnation and Redemption'. She experienced salvation. She experienced the fruit of her prayer 'Hallowed be thy name'. God's name was hallowed in Jane, not by anything she did, but by what he did.

At the close of this chapter I suggest that you take a little time to pray over the text of Ezekiel 36 on the new heart. As you prayerfully read this promise note the following: God's name is hallowed not by what we do, but by what he does. God's name is hallowed when we receive the 'new heart'. God's name is made holy when we allow God to 'pour clean water' over us and cleanse us from all defilement.

Faith sharing

1. In the past what did you understand by the phrase 'hallowed be thy name'?
2. In what area of your own life have you experienced the gift of the new heart?
3. God promises in Ezekiel to 'cleanse us from our idols'. Sometimes the idol may be a job, or a promotion. Has anything ever tended to become an idol in your own life? Can you recall how you were 'cleansed' from it?
4. If you were in Jane's position what would you be expecting God to do as you prayed 'hallowed be thy name'?

Scripture reading

The daily systematic reading of the New Testament prepares your heart and mind to hear and receive the word of God. The Vatican Council tells us how to read the sacred Scriptures: 'Let them remember, however, that prayer should accompany the reading of the sacred Scriptures, so that a dialogue takes place between God and man. For, we speak to him when we pray; we listen to him when we read the sacred scriptures.[11]

At the end of each chapter of this book I will give a reading list for the week. If you follow this list you will read the whole of the New Testament in twelve weeks.

Sunday	Matthew 1—3
Monday	Matthew 4—6
Tuesday	Matthew 7—9
Wednesday	Matthew 10—12
Thursday	Matthew 13—14
Friday	Matthew 15—17
Saturday	Matthew 18—20

2

Living by the word of God

In her long night of prayer, as she praised God with 'all that is within' Jane found that her whole being was integrated. She experienced a profound healing. She also discovered the truth of Christ's words that 'humans do not live on bread alone but on every word that comes from the mouth of God' (Matt. 4:4). The gift of the new heart, which we seek as we pray 'hallowed be thy name', enables us to hear the word of God, to accept it and to begin to live by it.

Each of us has had the experience of 'living by a word'. Sometimes, of course, we have never reflected on this experience. Recall, for instance, an occasion when you were feeling in great form: everything was going well; you had no worries; the family were well; you had good friends. Then, out of the blue, a person whom you considered a good friend said something, or did something nasty to you. What happened? You probably spent the rest of the day thinking about it, worrying about it, getting mad about it. Your whole mood changed. From feeling elated you began to feel deflated. What was happening? You had begun to live by the nasty word. That is the power of the human word. It can build up or it can pull down; it can elate or deflate; it can encourage or discourage.

Our protection against the destructive, sinful human word is the creative, liberating word of God. We must consciously choose that protection. If we wish we can ignore God's word and live simply by the human word. In this chapter I want to consider some of the implications of living by God's word. But first of all, we have to consider what is involved in living by the word.

Formation of self-image

Our self-image is formed by a word. That is the most profound influence the word exercises in our life. None of us is born with a self-image. When the baby is born it has no awareness of being separate from its mother. It gradually comes to the awareness of its separate identity. The identity which the baby begins to form for itself is at the mercy of the words spoken to it: beautiful or ugly, welcome or unwelcome, a joy or a nuisance.

As the words of love or rejection, of affirmation or repudiation enter into the baby's consciousness, its self-image is formed. The baby will grow up as a confident, assured young person, capable of trusting and reaching out in love to others, or as an insecure, self-centred young person, incapable of reaching out in real love to others. Parents are becoming more and more aware of the need to speak lovingly, affirmingly and positively to their children. In those early stages of development the child's self-image is formed by those words.

In this chapter, however, we are not concerned with the words which parents and family speak to the young children. We are concerned with the words which the adult person speaks to himself or herself. We are concerned with our self-talk. As we mature, our self-image comes under the influence of our own self-talk. What are we saying to ourselves about ourselves? Are we proclaiming to ourselves God's liberating word of love and acceptance or are we speaking to ourselves our own sinful word of condemnation and rejection? We form our self-image as adults either by our own sinful self-talk, in which we forever find fault with ourselves, or by God-talk in which we allow the word of God to enter into our consciousness. My real identity is not revealed by finding out who I am in my own sinful eyes but in coming to understand who I am in God's loving and forgiving eyes.

Jane described her struggle in making this discovery in this way: 'It was very painful and humbling to discover that the

God whom I had moved away from still loved and cared for me. It was fierce struggling and tremendous pain to raise one's head bent in shame and meet the eyes of forgiveness and love.' As she grappled with that pain her self-image was transformed. The self-image controls the way we feel about ourselves. Recall the self-image which Jane so vividly described. She said Fr P who helped her on the road to recovery 'met an angry, foul mouthed, depressed woman – to the point that I felt suicidal, dead and empty within'. Her story, which explained how she was feeling was 'wrapped in fear and guilt and somehow sealed with silence'. She knew that there was an intimate connection between the way she saw herself and the way she was feeling about herself. As she said, 'God forgave me long before I was able to forgive myself'. Her self-image dictated the way she saw herself. That self-image was formed not by what God said to her about herself but by what she was saying to herself about herself. And because she was acutely aware of the sin she had committed through having the abortion she was condemning herself. Hating herself. Even contemplating destroying herself.

She was living by her guilt and fear. She was able to say with the psalmist, 'Down in the dust I lie prostrate', but in the midst of her shame and guilt she was not able to say, 'revive me as your word has guaranteed' (Ps. 119:25). Jane's self-image was not being formed by the creative word of God; it was being formed by the destructive word of shame and guilt. She used the colourful phrase 'I had locked myself up in fear, shame and guilt' to describe that inner house in which she dwelt. Her phrase for her captivity evokes Jesus' image for true freedom: 'If you make my word your home you will indeed be my disciples, you will learn the truth and the truth will set you free' (John 8:31).

Jesus uses the image of 'home' when he speaks about his word. His word is the home in which we are invited to dwell. Taking up our residence in this home of God's word guarantees our freedom. Home is where you know your true identity. You are a son or daughter of the house. We would never speak of 'being locked up' at home. Jane could speak about being 'locked up in fear, shame and guilt'. She was in the prison of the destructive word, not in the home of God's creative word. Because her self-image was being formed in that prison she could say that 'inside me was cursing, hate, anger and destruction'. She needed liberation and she could not free herself. As her merciful Father completed her liberation from her prison of hate and despair during the Mass she found her true home in God's word. She spent the whole night before God praying 'let all that is within me cry worthy'. And she recognised the providential significance of this. She wrote: 'This, for me, was to complete the healing, because in all of it, I would have felt unworthy of what the good Lord was doing in me.'

She had lived so long in that prison of the destructive word, condemning herself even though she was sorry for her sins, that she found it difficult to believe that God could love or esteem her. She needed the whole night in prayer to enter into true freedom. In the Mass, that afternoon, we gave a lot of time to the prayer 'We thank you for counting us worthy to stand in your presence and serve you'. It is God himself who declares us worthy. She filled the whole night with that prayer. She had come home. As she said, 'I am eternally grateful to the students and the staff who encouraged, supported and enabled me to make the journey, a journey into the embrace of God's love and forgiveness and the gift of baby Pat.'

Jane discovered the truth about God revealed in the prophet Isaiah:

> Let her turn back to Yahweh who will take pity on her,
> to our God who is rich in forgiving;
> for my thoughts are not your thoughts,
> my ways are not your ways – it is Yahweh who speaks.
> Yes, the heavens are as high above earth
> as my ways are above your ways,
> my thoughts above your thoughts. (Isa. 55:8–9)

In her all night vigil of prayer and praise Jane discovered how different God is from us. As Jürgen Moltmann wrote:

OUR THOUGHTS ARE THOUGHTS OF JUDGEMENT. WE ARE forsaken. We are forgotten. We have no future, our anxiety tells us. The thoughts of God are not like our thoughts. Our ways under the law we keep are not his ways. We condemn ourselves, but he does not condemn us. We are resigned to our fate, but he is not. We judge ourselves and others according to the iron law of reciprocity; but his is a law of 'much forgiveness'. Therein God is – no actually becomes different.[1]

The image of two houses

In the Scripture we have the striking image of two quite different 'houses' in which we can make home. Jesus invites us to make home in his word (John 8:31). In the psalms we are warned about the destructive word: 'you love the destructive word, you tongue of deceit' (Ps. 52:4).

If our self-image is formed in the house of the destructive word we will have a very poor self-image. We will have a low esteem of ourselves and a low esteem of everyone else as well. If we discover that we have taken up residence in the house of destructive word, if we find that we are negative about ourselves and others, then it is most urgent that we vacate that house immediately. We abandon the house of the destructive word and make home in God's word. That transition is a good image for inner healing. Inner healing is the experience of the healing love of God in which the person realises that self is lovable (healing of the self-image) or that self can love and forgive others (healing of relationships) or that self can gratefully integrate some painful past event into the present (healing of memories). Each of these healings comes through faithfully living by the word of God. We will consider each type of healing in turn.

27

Healing of self-image

Scripture says that God 'sent forth his word and he healed them' (Ps. 105:20). All healing comes through the word of God. As we live by the word that God speaks for our healing, his affirming word about ourselves, we escape the prison of the destructive word. The very first word which God speaks about us is, 'let us make man in our own image, in the likeness of ourselves. So God made man in the image of himself, male and female he created them' (Gen. 1:26). We are then told that God blessed them. When he saw all that he had made he declared that it was 'very good'. In this story of our creation we are told the good news about ourselves. When God made us he modelled us on himself – his own image and likeness. You may have been enchanted by beautiful scenery, enthralled by wonderful sunsets, inspired by great works of art. But, nothing in all creation, no matter how beautiful, is more like God than ourselves. As Scripture says: 'We are God's work of art, created in Christ Jesus, to live the good life as he intended us to live it from the beginning' (Eph. 2:9).

God not only tells us that he created us in his own image and likeness. He tells us how he feels about us. He says: 'you are precious in my sight and I love you and give you honour. Do not be afraid I have redeemed you' (Isa. 43:10). How do you feel in the presence of someone who keeps telling you that you are precious in his or her sight? God keeps telling us 'I have loved you with an everlasting love' (Jer. 31:3). God addressed all our emotions. He tells us not to fear (366 times), that we will not be put to shame (Ps. 71:1), that he will protect us and deliver us (Ps. 109:21) that we are the apple of his eye (Zech. 2:12), that he exults with joy over us. As we go through the Bible we find hundreds of divine protestations of undying love. The one that sums up all the others is surely Christ's own words: 'God loved the world so much that he gave up his only Son, so that everyone who believes in him may not be lost but may have eternal life' (John 3:16).

So often there is a massive discrepancy between the word God speaks to us about ourselves and the way we feel about ourselves. God says we are redeemed, we feel we are lost; God says he loves us with an everlasting love, we feel that he has never loved us at all; God says we are precious in his sight, we feel that we are of very little value to him; God says that he will give us a new heart and put a new spirit in us, we feel that he can do nothing for us.

Where does this discrepancy come from? It originates in that destructive word, the sinful word about ourselves, which we receive into our consciousness and through which we form our self-image. It is true, of course, that we are sinners. We are fallen creatures. Made in the glorious image of God we rejected God. The Bible tells us graphically about the immediate effect of sin: 'The man and the woman heard the sound of the Lord God in the garden and they hid from the Lord God' (Gen. 3:8). Created and called to walk in God's presence Adam and Eve are now hiding themselves from his presence. They want to escape from God. But God will not simply let them walk away and hide. He calls out to them: 'Where are you'? Adam then confesses: 'I heard the sound of you in the garden, I was afraid because I was naked, so I hid' (Gen. 3:10). Our first parents had fallen from the heaven of God consciousness into the hell of self-consciousness.

They became aware of their nakedness and felt frightened in the presence of God. So they hid. All generations have suffered the consequences of this sin. As the *Catechism of the Catholic Church* says:

ONLY THE LIGHT OF DIVINE REVELATION CLARIFIES THE reality of sin and particularly of the sin committed at mankind's origins. Without the knowledge Revelation gives us of God we cannot recognise sin clearly and are tempted to explain it as merely a developmental flaw, a psychological weakness, a mistake, or a necessary consequence of an inadequate social structure, etc. Only in the knowledge of God's plan for man can we grasp that sin is an abuse of the freedom that God gives to created persons so that they are capable of loving him and loving one another.[2]

We cannot make sense of our human experience without confronting the reality of sin. Sin exists because of the freedom we enjoy in our relationship with God. We have been created for a life of union with God and we can use our freedom to choose a life apart from God. We choose this separation because we believe an illusion, the illusion that living outside God's law will bring us freedom and happiness.

The experience of sin brings the very opposite – fear, unhappiness, lack of freedom. Scripture says: 'the law of the Lord is perfect, it gives life to the soul' (Ps. 19:7). The illusion of sin says if you want real life ignore the law of the Lord. The discrepancy between what God says to us about ourselves and how we so often feel about ourselves can only be explained by this reality of sin in our lives.

Sin is alienation – alienation from God, from neighbour and from ourselves. Sin inflicts a wound in the self-image which leads to self-rejection. Conversion of heart brings not only forgiveness of sin but also the healing of the wound of sin. Pope Paul VI identified the healing of the wound of sin as the effect of the sacrament of reconciliation. He said, 'In order that this sacrament of healing may achieve its purpose in the life of an individual it must become deeply rooted in their lives and lead to more fervent love of God and neighbour.' Then he identified what is healed: 'Just as the wound of sin is varied and multiple in the life of an individual and of a community so too the healing which penance provides is varied.'[3]

We confess our sins; we acknowledge that 'the law of the Lord is perfect, it gives life to the soul' (Ps. 19:7) and we recognise that there can be no human happiness, no human fulfilment outside the law of God. The decision to live by every word that comes from the mouth of God always involves the decision to live by God's life-giving commandments. Agnes Stanford used to say that when we speak of sin as 'breaking God's law' we are not speaking correctly. We cannot break

God's law. If a man, she said, steps off the top of a precipice he doesn't break the law of gravity; he just demonstrates it! If we collide with the divine law that collision will not break God's law, it will break us.

The wound of sin in the self-image leads to self-rejection. The healing of that wound comes through the grace of self-acceptance. Self-acceptance, as Guardini said, is 'the foundation of all existence'. It is the goal of Christian existence. It is not there by birth, but by our rebirth. As St Peter said: 'your new birth was not from any mortal seed but from the everlasting word of the living and eternal God' (1 Pet. 1:23). If we wish to form our self-image by the word of God we must begin, like Mary the mother of Jesus and 'ponder God's word' in our heart.

God says to us: 'you are precious in my sight and I love you and give you honour' (Isa. 43:10); 'I love you with an everlasting love' (Jer. 31:3); Jesus says to us: 'you are the salt of the earth, you are the light of the world' (Matt. 5:13, 14). Our self-image must be formed by these divine words of affirmation and encouragement. The healing of our self-image takes place, and God's name is hallowed, as we confess our sins, ask God's pardon and then humbly begin to make God's word our home and forsake that house of the destructive word. We begin to live in the awareness that we are precious in God's sight, that we are loved with an everlasting love, that we are endowed with great dignity and worth. In the words of an old song we can 'walk tall and look the whole world in the eye'.

Healing of relationships

Living by the word of God, by the word of forgiveness, is the only way to experience healing for the inner wounds which are inflicted on us in our ordinary relationships with friends and acquaintances. Our instinct, when hurt, is to get 'even', to get our own back, which means simply to get revenge. St Peter asked Jesus: 'Lord how often must I forgive my brother if he wrongs me? As often as seven times? Jesus answered, not seven times, I tell you, but seventy-seven times' (Matt. 18:21). We must now live by that word. The word of God asks us to offer unconditional forgiveness; the word of our own hurt instinct asks for revenge. It is a choice between the word of God, which is the wisdom of God, or the word of our hurt feelings, which is the 'wisdom of this world'. Jesus asks us to forgive unconditionally because he is the man who, from the cross, could pray 'Father forgive them, they do not know what they are doing' (Luke 23:34).

Judged by the wisdom of this world, unconditional forgiveness is folly, but it belongs to the 'folly of the cross'. As St Paul said:

DO YOU SEE HOW GOD HAS SHOWN UP THE FOOLISHNESS OF human wisdom? If it was God's wisdom that human wisdom should not know God, it was because God wanted to save those who have faith through the foolishness of the message we preach. And so, while the Jews demand miracles and the Greeks look for wisdom, here are we preaching a crucified Christ; to the Jews an obstacle that they cannot get over, to the pagans madness, but to those who have been called, whether they are Jews or Greeks, a Christ who is the power of God and the wisdom of God. (1 Cor. 1:21–24)

It is the crucified Jesus, the God-man who was insulted, betrayed, rejected and finally executed on a cross, who teaches us to forgive unconditionally, who tells us 'to love our enemies'. Christ's teaching on forgiveness has never been popular. Is his teaching on 'unconditional forgiveness' the wisdom of God? It is only when we firmly believe that 'the crucified Christ' is 'the power of God and the wisdom of God' that we will be able to proclaim that unconditional forgiveness too is the wisdom of God. Such forgiveness takes its meaning from the cross. We cannot harmonise in our faith an acceptance of the crucified Christ with a rejection of his words 'Father forgive'. The quality of my faith acceptance of Christ crucified, the wounded, suffering, dying Jesus, is clearly manifested in the quality of the unconditional forgiveness which I offer to a brother or a sister.

Through forgiving we truly accept the Christ who was wounded and died for us and we experience the truth proclaimed in Scripture: 'By his wounds you have been healed.' (1 Pet. 2:24; cf. Isa. 53:5). Unconditional forgiveness heals the broken heart.

Forgiveness must never be confused with condoning or excusing. C. S. Lewis wrote:

> THERE IS ALL THE DIFFERENCE IN THE WORLD BETWEEN forgiving and excusing. Forgiveness says, 'Yes, you have done this thing, but I accept your apology, I will never hold it against you and everything between us two will be exactly the same as it was before.' But excusing says, 'I see that you couldn't help it, or didn't mean it, you weren't really to blame.' If one was not really to blame then there is nothing to forgive. In this sense forgiveness and excusing are almost opposite.[4]

When we forgive the person who has hurt us from our heart we are exercising the mighty power of God's word, living by his word, and through that word the broken heart is healed.

In one of her dialogues with God the Father, St Catherine of Siena asked him what did he really think of the person who forgave a wrong from the heart? God responded: 'That person has become divine.' God's name is truly hallowed in us when we forgive. Unconditional forgiveness is a divine reality. As we enter into this divine reality of unconditional forgiveness we in turn are divinised. When we receive this grace of forgiveness and when we offer it to the person who has wronged us we ourselves are 'graced' by the divine forgiveness we offer. In that very act of forgiving we are divinised. We become like the Father. That is what Jesus asks when he says: 'Be compassionate as your heavenly father is compassionate' (Luke 6:36).

We see the power of forgiveness in the life of Nelson Mandela. From the day he was released from prison the man who was locked up for nearly thirty years as a 'violent communist and a dangerous revolutionary' has been preaching the truly revolutionary message of reconciliation, calling on his own people, the oppressed and long-suffering black majority of

South Africa, to forgive their white oppressors. Mandela sees clearly that it is not only the oppressed who need liberation; the oppressor is also in need of liberation. Reconciliation is the only road which leads to liberation. In his autobiography he tells us how he fought the spiritual battle to survive as a freedom fighter in prison: 'Prison is designed to break one's spirit and destroy one's resolve. To do this the authorities attempt to exploit every weakness, demolish every initiative, negate all sign of individuality – all with the idea of stamping out that spark that makes each of us human and each of us who we are.'[5] That spark which makes us human is the image of God within us. Mandela understood clearly that if the prison authorities could make him hate they would have broken his spirit. He was a prisoner for justice not for revenge. He tells us about his experience when he stood as a prisoner in the court room where he had, as a lawyer, defended many people:

> DURING THE PROCEEDINGS, THE MAGISTRATE WAS DIFFIDENT and uneasy, and would not look at me directly. The other attorneys also seemed embarrassed, and at that moment I had something of a revelation. These men were not only uncomfortable because I was a colleague brought low, but because I was an ordinary man being punished for his beliefs. In a way I had never quite comprehended before, I realised the role I could play in court and the possibilities before me as a defendant. I was a symbol of justice in the court of the oppressor, the representative of the great ideals of freedom, fairness and democracy in a society that dishonoured those virtues. I realised then and there that I could carry on the fight even within the fortress of the enemy.[6]

By keeping his spirit free from bitterness and unforgiveness Mandela did that. For nearly thirty years from prison he inspired the struggle for freedom and justice in South Africa. He remained a free man in prison – free from hatred, from bitterness, from the desire for revenge. Today he is the first president of all South Africans.

Healing of memories

Sad memories from the past, hidden resentments, even bitterness can be the source of great pain and discouragement. How do we live according to the word of God with regard to the past? How do we relate to our past? The word which God gives us is clear and simple direction: 'Bless Yahweh, my soul, bless his holy name, all that is within me! Bless Yahweh, my soul, and never forget all his blessings' (Ps. 103:1–2). The word of God invites us to bless God not just with our minds, not just with our hearts or spirits, but with 'all that is within me'. What is within me? Everything that has ever happened to me in my whole life is within me, stored in that faculty which we call memory. The human memory is like a computer. Every single thing which happens in life is fed into that computer. Most of the events are registered in the subconscious; but every single event is registered. The question is: what are all those millions of human experiences doing in my life? I know that I am the person I am today because of the things which I have lived through – my early years in my family, as I grew up; my primary and secondary education; my formation as a priest and a Redemptorist; the 31 years I have spent in priestly ministry. Those were the major formative influences in my life. There were also deforming influences: my own sinfulness; the discouragement which I experienced from time to time; my failure to pursue my own ongoing formation; the hurts and disappointments and frustrations which are part of life in a fallen world.

With regard to all those experiences, both positive and negative, I have to live according to the word of God. That word directs me to bless God with and in and through all those experiences. It is easy to bless God for the good experiences. But before I can bless God for the bad experiences I need healing. Specifically, I need the healing of memories. What kind of memory do I have as I recall the negative influences, the hurts and the disappointments? The answer to this question shows whether I am living by the word of God or living by the destructive word. The word of God says: 'all that is within me bless.' The destructive word, with regard to those negative or painful influences would say: 'all that is within me curse.'

If I find that I am filled with resentments or bitterness as I recall those events I know I am living by the destructive word: I am wounded, imprisoned in the house of the destructive word. Healing and liberation come through living by God's word. For all those past, negative influences I should pray 'all that is within me bless, all those negative influences from my past bless, all those disappointments and frustrations from the past, bless'. If the past within me is not blessing God it will be cursing; it will remain un-integrated into my present existence and will be a source of deep unhappiness. I will have bitter and resentful memories.

God wants us to have grateful memories. He does not want us to be burdened with resentful memories. Yet, so many people go through life, filled with resentments about the past. The word 'resent' comes from the Latin word *re-sentire* which means 'to feel again'. When we nourish a resentful memory we 'feel again' the hurt from the past. It will remain a wound within until it is healed. Time does not heal inner wounds. The only way to have that wound healed is to live by the word of God and say 'all that is within me bless God's holy name'.

When Jesus says that we do not live 'on bread alone but on every word that comes from the mouth of God' he gives us the secret for living in peace – in peace with ourselves because we can pray 'we thank you for the wonder of my being', in peace with our neighbour because we can 'forgive seventy times seven' and at peace with our past life because we can pray 'let all that is within us bless God's holy name'. Living by these life giving words of God we experience inner healing and we become peaceful people. God's name is hallowed.

Faith sharing

1. Is your self-image formed in the house of God's creative word or in the house of the destructive, sinful word?
2. Have you consciously set out to live by God's word which declares that you are 'very good' and 'precious in God's sight'?
3. Can you share two examples to illustrate:

   a) how living by the destructive word made you feel bad and destructive?

   b) how living by the creative word of God made you feel good and creative?

Scripture reading

The Second Vatican Council says: 'The Church has always venerated the divine Scriptures as she venerated the Body of the Lord.'[7] We approach our reading of the Scriptures with great reverence, just as we approach the Blessed Sacrament with great reverence. Before you begin your reading always spend a moment in prayer, asking God the Father to fill you with the Holy Spirit so that you will hear his Word.

Sunday	Matthew 22—23
Monday	Matthew 24—28
Tuesday	Mark 1—2
Wednesday	Mark 3—5
Thursday	Mark 6—8
Friday	Mark 9—10
Saturday	Mark 11—13

3

Getting to
know the word of God

When the Second Vatican Council declared in 1963 that ignorance of the Scriptures is ignorance of Christ' it issued its greatest
challenge to the Catholic Church. The real challenge to the
Church in our times is not to get our Sunday congregations
singing and worshipping God in new and more joyful ways,
though that is surely most necessary. Nor is the real challenge
to get all the faithful actively involved in building up their
Christian communities, although such involvement is vital for
the future of the Church. The real challenge is getting to know
Christ personally, the knowledge that St Paul craved for when
he said: 'I believe nothing can outweigh the supreme advantage
of knowing Christ Jesus my Lord' (Phil. 3:9). When the Vatican
carried out an extensive study on why Catholics are leaving
the Church to join other Churches it gave this recommendation:
'Special attention should be given to the experiential dimension
of our faith, i.e. discovering Christ personally through prayer
and dedication (e.g. the charismatic and born-again
movements).'[1] This personal knowledge of Christ is a precious
gift of God. To acquire it, we must be willing to deal with that
basic ignorance of the Scripture which so many of us have.

Word of God

We believe that the Scriptures are the word of God. In order
to speak to us human beings, and thus reveal himself to us,
God choose to speak in human language. We would not be
able to understand any other language. As the Vatican Council

said, 'Indeed the words of God, expressed in the words of men, are in every way like human language, just as the Word of the eternal Father, when he took to himself the flesh of human weakness, became like men.'[2]

The mystery of God's word spoken through human words is similar to the mystery of God acting through human flesh and blood. Jesus Christ is fully human and fully divine. When Jesus speaks as a man, God is also speaking. In the same way the word of Scripture which we hear proclaimed in our Church, as the human word of St Paul or the prophet Jeremias, is also the word of God.

Incarnation and inspiration

We call the mystery of God entering into our human flesh and becoming man, the mystery of the incarnation. We call the fact that in and through the human words, which we find in Scripture, God speaks to us, the mystery of inspiration. The Vatican Council expounded this mystery in this way: 'To compose the sacred books, God chose certain men who, all the while he employed them in this task, made full use of their own faculties and powers so that, though he acted in them and by them, it was as true authors that they consigned to writing whatever he wanted written, and no more.'[3]

The inspiration of the Bible does not mean that God dictated the Bible. When St Paul sat down to write a letter to the church of Corinth, he was not acting as God's secretary, writing down every word that God said to him. Paul said to the Corinthians what he himself wanted to say. He knew their situation; he had founded the church in Corinth; he knew all about their gifts and their vices. And he wrote to them about all these things. Paul was making use of 'his own faculties and powers', saying what he wanted to say. For proper understanding of the letters of St Paul, or indeed of any of the other books of the Bible, we have to understand what the human author was saying. What is Paul trying to communicate to the Corinthians or to the Romans? As Gerald O'Collins says:

THE DIVINE AUTHORITY IMPARTED TO THE SCRIPTURES through divine inspiration in no way exempts interpreters (including preachers) from the serious task of establishing the meaning intended by the human authors. The special grace of inspiration did not violate the natural talents and limits of the biblical writers. We hear the voice of God through their voice. The word of God comes to us through the words of human beings. While recognising the divine authority of the scriptural texts, Christian preachers must still labour at understanding the meaning intended by the human author of these texts – that is to say, what they wished to communicate when they wrote what they did for the audiences they had in mind. Their meaning did not (and does not) coincide in a simplistic way with the explicit wording they adopted. The literary and religious conventions of their time are indispensable guides in establishing, with greater or less success, what the biblical writers intended to say when they used the words they did.[4]

The Catholic Church has always held biblical study in high esteem. This study of the sacred texts of Scripture – the style of language used, the meaning of the symbolism for the original hearers of the word, the whole historical context in which the sacred texts were written – is vital for a correct interpretation of the word in each new situation and each new culture. This does not mean, however, that only biblical scholars can read the Bible. The Bible is for each person, not just for the learned scholars. But the biblical scholars can help us understand the word of God more accurately by enabling us to understand the human word more correctly. Since we believe that the word of Scripture is the word of God we must do everything we can to correctly understand that word. The Vatican Council expresses our faith in the Scriptures in this way: 'Since therefore all that the inspired authors or sacred writers affirm should be regarded as affirmed by the Holy Spirit, we must acknowledge that the books of Scripture firmly, faithfully, and without error teach that truth which God, for the sake of our salvation, wished to see confided to the Sacred Scriptures.'[5]

The Council says that 'ignorance of the Scriptures is ignorance of Christ' because Scripture is the eternal word of God who came among us in the flesh, Jesus Christ our Lord. The *Catechism of the Catholic Church* puts it this way: 'Through all the words of Sacred Scripture, God speaks only one single Word, his one Utterance in whom he expresses life to the soul' (Ps. 19:7). And quoting St Augustine it continues: 'You recall that one and the same Word of God extends throughout Scripture, that it is one and the same Utterance that resounds in the mouths of all the sacred writers, since he who was in the beginning God with God has no need of separate syllables: for he is not subject to time.'[6] Each book of the Bible, in its own way, is speaking God's Word to us. As the Council said, 'In the sacred books, the Father who is in heaven comes lovingly to meet his children, and talks with them.'[7]

Love of the Scriptures

In 1967 when I joined the staff in our seminary to teach I was amazed to discover that the man who had taught me Scripture as a student, a highly qualified biblical scholar, could not accept much of what the Council said about the word of God. He found the statement that 'the Church has always venerated the Scripture as she venerates the Lord's Body' quite unacceptable. While he believed that Scripture was the inspired word of God he could not accept that there was any real comparison between the Sacrament of the Lord's Body and the proclamation of the Word. The 'real presence' of Christ in the word should not, in his view, be compared with the 'real presence' of Christ in the Sacrament. Catholics, he would say, have a devotion to Christ in the Blessed Sacrament but not to Christ in the word. He found 'bible services' poor and unacceptable alternatives to Rosary and Benediction. Yet the Church's position is very clear: 'When the sacred scriptures are read in the church, God himself is speaking to his people, and Christ, present in his word, is proclaiming his Gospel.'[8] The bishops of the Second Vatican Council were well aware that many Catholics, even for centuries, did not have any real devotion to the word of God. That is why they reached the conclusion that 'it is essential to promote that sweet and living love for sacred scripture to which the venerable tradition of Eastern and Western rites gives testimony'.[9] It is not sufficient to have a knowledge of the Scriptures; we should have 'a sweet and living love' for them. Even theologians who were very concerned to understand Catholic doctrine in the light of the Scriptures, did not always have this devotional reverence for the Bible. In my own training as a theologian I learned to use the Scriptures for apologetic purposes. I could prove Catholic doctrine from the Scriptures. In a sense the Scriptures were a vast quarry from which we learned to hew 'proof texts' or useful texts for preaching. We were trained to prove the Church's teaching on the Mass and the sacraments by referring to specific parts of Scripture; we could prove that the doctrine of the Holy Trinity is revealed in the Scriptures; we could demonstrate that the Scriptures prove that Christ is the Son of God and that he founded the Church. But we were not trained to have a 'sweet and living love' for the Scriptures.

This 'sweet and living love' which so many Catholics now have for the word of God is the great grace of renewal which the Holy Spirit has poured out upon the Church through the Second Vatican Council. We find this love for the Scriptures especially among those who have been touched by renewal in the Spirit. One old priest testified to this grace when he said that before he became involved in renewal in the Spirit the Scriptures in his office book were like a dead letter. Now, he said, 'my office book, is like a box of chocolates. I am for ever dipping into it'. We should ask the Lord for the grace of true devotion to the word of God. A busy missionary sister describes how she came to have a love for the Scriptures:

I WAS A WORKAHOLIC. AS FULL TIME TEACHER AND boarding mistress in a mission school in Africa, my day was full. In such a situation my prayer and spiritual duties got second place – often left till late at night when I would be too tired to concentrate. Then in 1974 I made a Directed Retreat on the Spiritual Exercises of St Ignatius. During the hours of prayer on the scriptures each day the Lord became very close to me. In an overwhelming way, I became aware of his great love for me and I began to realise what I had been missing in my 'busy life' heretofore. I resolved that this would change. That was 20 years ago. By God's grace I have not lost my love for the word of God and my periods of prayer are the most important times of the day.

God wants to give each of us that same love for his holy word. But, we must give him time.

Commitment

If you have not been a regular reader of the Scriptures you may feel that it is now too late to begin or you may feel that the Bible is such a big, complicated book that you do not know where to begin. First of all it is never too late to begin the prayerful reading of the Scriptures. Each day you read the Scriptures you are hearing God's voice, getting to know Christ in a new way. And the converse is true. Each day you do not open the Scriptures is a day when you have not met the Lord where he wants to meet us, namely in his word. As the Council said, 'In the sacred books the Father who is in heaven comes lovingly to meet his children, and talks with them.'[10] In our Scripture reading we enter into a conversation with God the Father. That is the source of all prayer and the source too of our spiritual life. In the words of the Council: 'Such is the force and power of the Word of God that it can serve the Church as her support and vigour, and the children of the Church as strength for their faith, food for the soul, and a pure and lasting fount of spiritual life.'[11] Just as our physical life will not remain strong and robust without our daily food, so our spiritual life will not become strong without our daily visit to the 'pure and lasting fount'.

Daily Scripture reading demands a very definite decision on our part and a strong commitment to be faithful to the decision. We must have a definite time set aside for our daily reading. If I don't have a definite time for my reading I don't do it. I may have the good intention of a daily reading, but I have discovered over and over again that when the time is not clearly fixed, specified and set aside, the reading does not take place. On the other hand, I know when a specific time is clearly identified as 'my Scripture reading time' I do it and enjoy doing it. Those who have followed the spiritual formation programme on our missions testify to the same. Part of the programme is the daily reading of the New Testament. I have identified the reading for each day of the twelve week programme. The reading takes about fifteen minutes. During the twelve week programme, with fifteen minutes devoted to reading each day, the person reads the whole of the New Testament in twelve weeks. Margaret writes about her experience of daily reading of the New Testament:

BY BEING A MEMBER OF A 'FAITH SHARING GROUP' I FELT committed to really wanting to read the New Testament on a daily basis. It made me more aware of what Our Father wanted to do in my life; it enabled me to reach out to others with love and compassion; it helped all of us to become more Christlike. All the people in our group hoped that the faith sharing groups would continue in some sort of way as we had so much to share about how God worked in our lives every day.

Phyllis Gallacher shared a similar reflection on her experience of sharing Scripture and faith in a small group:

IN THE PROGRAMME 'HALLOWED BE THY NAME' I WAS A group leader. In the small group I found a great response. It encouraged the reading of Scripture and prayer. The sharing was very good and everyone brought their own personal experience and understanding. As time went on we became more open and able to share more deeply. I think it was an excellent way of sharing our faith.

Several aspects of these two testimonies are worth highlighting:

- The group enhanced commitment to daily reading of the New Testament.
- Daily reading made them more aware of what God the Father wanted to do in their life.
- Daily reading helped them to reach out with love and compassion.
- People bring their own personal experience to reading the New Testament and this enriches the sharing and understanding of the faith.
- People discover that their sharing deepens as time goes on and they want the group to continue: as Margaret said, 'we had so much to share about how God worked in our lives every day.'

Fifteen minutes a day is about the right length of time to give to your daily reading. First of all, out of the one thousand, four hundred and forty minutes in each day you can find fifteen minutes for your daily reading. In a moment of enthusiasm this might seem far too little. You might want to give a few hours. We must beware of enthusiasms. If you begin by saying that for the rest of your life you will read the Bible for an hour or two each day you will not persevere. You may do it for a week or two; you will not be able to do it each day, each week, each year.

But, if you decide that you will devote fifteen minutes each day to reading the Scriptures and if you make a commitment to do this reading you will probably persevere. You will have the experience of missing a few days, maybe a few weeks. But then, you just start again. Never be disheartened by your failures.

Faith sharing

1. How does the Vatican Council's statement that 'ignorance of the Scripture is ignorance of Christ' make you feel?
2. What word of Christ in the Gospel spoke to you most clearly this week?
3. How do you feel about the task of getting to know the Scriptures?

Scripture reading

The Vatican Council says: 'In the sacred books the Father who is in heaven comes lovingly to meet his children, and talks with them'.[12] As you read the Scriptures this week always begin with the awareness that it is God the Father who is coming to speak with you.

Sunday	Mark 14—16
Monday	Luke 1
Tuesday	Luke 2—3
Wednesday	Luke 4—5
Thursday	Luke 6—7
Friday	Luke 8—9
Saturday	Luke 10—11

4

The word in prayer

Prayer is talking to God. Long before we get round to speaking to God, however, he has already spoken to us. Our biggest mistake when we go to pray is to speak to God about ourselves and our needs while ignoring completely what he has been saying to us. Our first word in prayer, if we want to be polite, should be a response to what God is saying. If you had spoken nice, complimentary words to a friend and he completely ignored what you said and proceeded to tell you all about himself you would probably feel that he was being very rude.

Prayer is a response to what God says to us. The old definition of prayer is still valid: prayer is lifting the mind and heart to God. But not to a silent God, nor to a God who has never spoken to us. We lift our mind and heart to God because we have heard what he says and we want to respond. We want to enter into a conversation with him. The Vatican Council's words can be our starting point: 'In the sacred scriptures the Father who is in heaven comes lovingly to meet his children and talks with them.'[1] It is the Father who begins the conversation. Recall how Adam, after he had sinned, wanted to escape from God's presence. He did not want to engage in a conversation with God. But God came looking for him. He called out in the garden 'where are you?' (Gen. 3:9). It is as if God was saying 'what's the matter with you, why don't you want to talk to me?' Notice that it is God who came looking for Adam; Adam did not go looking for God. In fact, he was hiding from God. Notice too that it is God who speaks first. Adam is holding his breath in fear and God takes the initiative: 'where are you?'

All human prayer is really a response to that call of God:

47

'here I am Lord, you have called me', would be a good way to begin any period of prayer. The Vatican Council said 'We speak to God when we pray; we listen to him when we read the scriptures.'[2] In every conversation there is a time for listening and a time for speaking. The good conversationalist is the one who has found the right balance between the two. Were you ever in the company of someone who never stopped talking? In the end you were probably not able to listen. Incessant talking impedes good listening. Perhaps you have also been in the company of someone who never says a word. He just sits there. In the end, no doubt, you were left wondering whether he had heard a word you said. The non-participation of the silent party makes it almost impossible to continue the conversation. Good conversation needs both good listening and good talking. Good prayer needs the same.

We must know how to listen to God; prayerful reading of the Scripture is the best way to listen to God. We must also be ready to respond to him when we hear his voice; for that our personal prayer is essential. A lady describes how her life was changed by listening to God:

BEFORE THE SCRIPTURES CAME ALIVE FOR ME I NEVER thought that Jesus accepted me as I am with my faults and failings – wanting in so many ways. I felt I could never repay him for his wonderful goodness and patience with me. I was so fearful. The day we gathered for a Prayer Meeting and prayed in groups for each other, expressing our need for healing, a wonderful peace and joy filled me. When again that evening we prayed in silence during Exposition a great peace descended upon me. I felt a different person and wanted to say with the apostles on the mountain, 'Lord it is good for us to be here'.

She had struggled for years at her prayers. But, as she says, 'I never thought that Jesus accepted me as I am'. She was not comfortable in the Lord's presence because she felt bad about herself. She felt that Jesus felt the same way about her as she felt about herself. That made a heart to heart conversation with the Lord impossible. Her prayer was full of duty and fear; it was very preoccupied with her own sinfulness. Because she could not really trust Jesus she could not forget about herself and her weaknesses. Her prayer lacked warmth, simplicity and love. Then, as she says, 'the Scriptures came alive for me'. Not only her prayer but her whole relationship with the Lord was transformed.

She was trying to pray without listening. God had spoken wonderful words of acceptance and love and she had failed to respond to them. God her Father had said to her, 'you are precious in my sight and I love you and give you honour, do not be afraid for I am with you' (Isa. 43:4); he had further revealed to her that 'The Lord is tender and compassionate, slow to anger, most loving' and that 'he never treats us, never punishes us, as our guilt and our sins deserve' (Ps. 103:8–10), but she ignored this revelation and lived with her fear of non-acceptance. Jesus had said to her, 'As the Father has loved me, so I have loved you' (John 15:9), but she had not heard him. And St Paul had reassured her with the words: 'The proof that you are children of God is that God has sent the Spirit of his Son in to our hearts: the Spirit that cries Abba, Father, and it is this that makes you a child, you are not a slave any more: and if God has made you child, then he has made you heir' (Gal. 4:6–7). But she went to her prayer as a slave, in fear of rejection. We all make this same mistake. So often we go to prayer, full of our own fears and anxieties, without listening, even for a moment, to what God is saying to us.

If a person was fearfully trying to find his way through a pitch black room, while refusing to switch on the light, we would find it hard to have much sympathy for his fears. We behave like that when we go to pray without the word of God. As the Scripture says, 'Your word is a lamp to my feet, a light on my path' (Ps. 118:105). If we embark in prayer on the dark roads of our life without this lamp we will become afraid of the dark, discouraged by our sinfulness and weakness and abandon our prayer very quickly. Our Lord taught this to St Jerome in a remarkable vision. Jerome had left everything to follow the Lord. He was living as hermit in a cave in Bethlehem. Our Lord appeared to him and said, 'Jerome, why don't you give me everything?' Jerome replied, 'but Lord I have given you everything. I gave up my career in Rome and came to live here as a hermit for your sake.' The Lord looked lovingly at Jerome and repeated his question: 'Jerome, why don't you give me everything?' In some agitation Jerome began to tell the Lord all he had given him: 'I gave up my house for you, my career in Rome, I am fasting until sunset and keeping vigils. What more can I give you?' The Lord thanked him kindly and said: 'Jerome, why don't you give me your sins?' The first thing we have to let go of, when we come into God's presence, is our sins. That is why it is so important, when we begin our prayer, to listen to God's word which always invites us to trust him with our sinfulness. As the Scriptures say:

SINCE IN JESUS, THE SON OF GOD, WE HAVE THE SUPREME high priest who has gone through to the highest heaven, we must never let go of the faith that we have professed. For it is not as if we had a high priest who was incapable of feeling our weaknesses with us; but we have one who has been tempted in every way that we are, though he is without sin. Let us be confident, then, in approaching the throne of grace, that we shall have mercy from him and find grace when we are in need of help. (Heb. 4:14–16)

St Hippolytus, writing in the third century said:

THERE IS ONE GOD, AND WE CAN COME TO KNOW HIM ONLY through the sacred scripture. So then, let us look at what scripture proclaims, let us discover what its teaching is. As the Father wants to be believed, so let us believe; as he wants his Son to be glorified, so let us glorify him; as he wants the Holy Spirit to be given, so let us receive him. We must not act in accordance with our own mind or our own will; we must not do violence to what God has given. We must look at things rather as God has chosen to make them known through scripture.[3]

When we go to pray it is necessary to see things as God sees them. That is seeing with 'the eye of faith'. We look out on a world that is full of violence and hatred and we hear the word about Jesus: 'Look, there is the lamb of God that takes away the sin of the world' (John 1:29). What do we want to talk to God about? Do we want to talk to him about the sin and wickedness of the world or do we want to thank him for Jesus who is the saviour of the world? Or, when we look into our own hearts and become aware of our own sinfulness we hear the words: 'Come now, let us talk this over, says Yahweh. Though your sins are like scarlet, they shall be as white as snow; though they are red as crimson, they shall be like wool' (Isa. 1:18). What should we be talking to God about? our sins or about how he makes them 'white as snow'? Without listening to the word of God in prayer we will focus simply on what is wrong, or on what we need, or on what we have to do. Without listening to God's word we can begin to pray in a way which denies God's great love and mercy. That kind of prayer fills us with fear and anxiety and robs us of peace and joy in God's presence. We should pray in the light of God's word and not in the darkness of our own fears.

Praying with the Scriptures

There are many ways in which we can pray with the Scriptures. I recommend three steps, especially while praying for inner healing: acceptance, acknowledgement and allowance.

ACCEPTANCE

When we begin our prayer we listen to what God is saying. God speaks an everlasting word. That means he does not have to repeat it. To each of us God says: 'You are precious in my sight and I love you and give you honour' (Isa. 43:4). Our first response to this word is to accept it. Acceptance of the word is not merely an intellectual assent. Acceptance involves total immersion in the word, the type of immersion Jesus implied when he said: 'If you make my word your home you will indeed me my disciples, you will learn the truth and the truth will make you free' (John 8:31–32). Jesus is saying that our relationship with the word of God must be similar to our relationship with our home. Feeling 'at home' means feeling comfortable, feeling accepted. Home is where you know who you are. You are a son or daughter of the house and you are accepted as such. You can relax. Jesus says: 'if you make my word your home you will indeed be my disciple.'

The first step in prayer is not simply to hear God's word but to enter into it, to dwell in it as you do in your own home. Then, Jesus says, you will receive a new identity: *you will be my disciples*. A disciple is one who listens to the master, who learns from the master, and who tries in every way to please the master. A disciple would never deny the master's word, or refuse to believe it. If the master says 'your sins are forgiven you' the disciple gratefully accepts his word. Pope John Paul II in his great encyclical on Christian morality describes what is involved in discipleship in this way: 'it involves holding fast to the very person of Jesus, partaking of his life and destiny, sharing in his free and loving obedience to the Father. By responding in faith and following the one who is Incarnate Wisdom, the disciple of Jesus truly becomes a disciple of God (John 6:45).'[4]

By identifying with Christ in this total and personal way we receive our new identity as his disciples. As disciples, dwelling in the word as in our home, we learn the truth. Truth is not something which we acquire through our own intellectual prowess. We have to learn it. The first condition for learning is docility, that is a willingness to be taught by the Master. Jesus is the Master and he teaches us the truth about our life and destiny. The Church of Christ, 'which upholds the truth and keeps it safe' (1 Tim. 3:14) faithfully interprets his teaching for us. As the Vatican Council said: 'The task of authentically interpreting the word of God, whether in its written form or of Tradition, has been entrusted only to those charged with the Church's living Magisterium, whose authority is exercised in the name of Jesus Christ.'[5] Dwelling in Christ's word always involves dwelling in the Church of Christ and being faithful to the teaching of the Church. The truth which we learn is preserved free from all error in the Church because the Church is the body of Christ. That is the truth which will set you free.

Dwelling as disciples in the word of God, as in our home, we learn the truth about God and the truth about God's relationship with us. Notice how detailed Jesus is when he speaks about the truth setting us free. It is not any truth that sets free. If someone is tone deaf and is told the truth that he or she cannot sing, that truth does not set free. It is the truth that we learn from God, as we dwell in God's word, which sets free. And the truth which God proclaims to us, as we come into his presence in prayer is 'you are precious in my sight and I love and give you honour' (Isa. 43:4). Hearing that word can transform our lives. At the end of a retreat to a large community of sisters one of the participants, a woman in her eighties got up and asked forgiveness from everyone in these graphic words: 'All my life I have been like a cat. Anyone who scratched me was scratched back in return. Now I know the reason: I never knew that I was precious in God's sight.' That truth set her free to relax in the presence of her sisters and in God's presence too. Until the day of her death I got a card from her on the anniversary of the retreat reminding me that she was still holding on to that liberating truth.

If we have taken the step which Jesus asks us to take, namely made his word our home, we will now be able to begin our heart to heart conversation with God. God has spoken first. He has assured you that you are very special to him. How are you going to respond? Pause for a moment right now and make your response. What a liberating truth to hold in your heart: you are precious in the sight of God.

The lady whose testimony I quoted in the last chapter talked about how fearful she was, how she could never really believe that Jesus accepted her as she was. The truth which God reveals to you is that he does accept you as you are and that it is as you are now that you are precious to him. You will not become precious to God when you become a better person, a holier person. You could not be more precious to God than you are right now. Your first response to this must be one of acceptance. Accept that this is the deepest truth about yourself in your relationship with God. The Holy Spirit inspired this response for our prayer:

> It was you who created my inmost self,
> who put me together in my mother's womb;
> for all these mysteries I thank you:
> for the wonder of myself, for the wonder of your works.
> (Ps. 139:13)

Use this response frequently in your prayer. When you have thanked God for the wonder of yourself you should then thank God for the wonder of all those in your life, especially those who may be causing you most trouble. Pause for a moment now and do that. Allow the people in your life to come into your mind and heart and thank God for them.

Notice how you felt as you thanked God for the wonder of yourself. Do not be surprised if you felt quite insincere or even if you felt incapable of saying the words at all. This response comes from the deep conviction that God created you with great love and that you are precious in his sight. If you have not got that deep conviction in your heart at this moment you will find it difficult to use these words in prayer. You would probably feel much more comfortable while saying 'Oh God be merciful to me a sinner', than while saying 'I thank you for the wonder of myself'. But, it is the same Holy Spirit who inspires both these responses. And the Holy Spirit, as St Paul assures us, is praying in us long before we get round to praying ourselves: 'The Spirit too comes to help us in our weakness. For when we cannot choose words to pray properly, the Spirit himself expresses our plea in a way that could never be put into words' (Rom. 8:26). Not only do we carry this praying Spirit in our hearts but at the right hand of the Father Jesus is also praying for us: 'He is living for ever to intercede for all who come to God through him' (Heb. 7:25). Tom Smail comments: 'Not only are *we being prayed for* by the ascended Son, *but we are being prayed in by the indwelling Spirit.* Perfect intercession is going on not only at the heart of heaven where Christ prays, but in our own heart where the Spirit prays.'[6] If you find it difficult, at this moment to pray 'Father, I thank you for the wonder of myself', let the Holy Spirit pray that prayer in you. Thank God that Jesus is saying that prayer for you in heaven. Then relax in the awareness that both Christ and the Spirit are interceding on your behalf at this very moment.

Now notice how you feel as you thank God for the wonder of your enemies. You have to say something to God about your enemies. Since your enemies are precious in God's sight, there would not be much point in you trying to turn God against them; nor would it make sense to ask God to change them and make them better people. That would be sitting in judgement on them. The only thing you can do with regard to your enemies is to act on the words of the Gospel. Jesus says to you: 'love your enemies and pray for those who persecute you' (Matt. 5:44). The most liberating and healing way to pray for your enemies is to thank God for the wonder of their being. This can be a most challenging prayer. But, as in your own case so in theirs: Christ and the Spirit are interceding *for* and *in* them too. Your attempt to thank God for the wonder of their being will indicate clearly whether you have, as yet, fully forgiven them. But, as you pray this prayer for your enemies you will get the grace to forgive. The hurts they have caused you will be healed and they will no longer have power over you.

ACKNOWLEDGEMENT

The second step in listening to God and using his word in our prayer is to acknowledge what he is doing in our life. Our Lady shows us the way. She knew how to ponder God's word in her heart. When Elizabeth praised her with the words, 'Of all women you are the most blessed', Mary responded in her Magnificat, 'the Almighty has done great things for me' (Luke 1:49). We are told the source of Elizabeth's word of praise: 'Now as soon as Elizabeth heard Mary's greeting, the child leapt in her womb and Elizabeth was filled with the Holy Spirit. She gave a loud cry and said "of all women you are the most blessed".' Elizabeth's word of praise comes from the Holy Spirit. It is the word of praise which, as it were, releases the Magnificat in Mary's heart. There is a Magnificat in each human heart and the heart will remain sad until it has sung it. Sometimes the heart has not sung its Magnificat because there is no Elizabeth to speak the word of praise. At other times, however, the word of praise has been spoken but the person refuses to accept it and refuses to acknowledge that the Almighty has done great things for him or her. Mary did not refuse the praise. She accepted it and acknowledged that God had done great things for her.

I sometimes ask a group of people to do this exercise. Take a page of paper. Make two columns by drawing a line down the middle. On the left hand column write down your ten best points. On the right hand column write down one or two, (if you can find that many!) points that are not so good. Invariably many in the group confess that while they had no problem in filling the right hand column with their negative points they found it very hard even to start on the left hand column with their positive points.

If a person cannot acknowledge the good things that God is doing in life he or she will not be able to enter into the prayer of praise. Mary's Magnificat is a prayer of perfect praise:

My soul proclaims the greatness of the Lord,
and my soul exults in God my saviour;
because he has looked upon his lowly handmaid.
Yes from this day forward all generations will call me blessed,
for the Almighty has done great things for me
Holy is his name. (Luke 1:47–50)

The good thing that God was doing in Mary's life led her to 'proclaim the greatness of God', not her own greatness, and 'to exult in God her saviour', not in herself. The good thing that God is doing in our lives should lead us to do the same thing.

C. S. Lewis said 'praise is inner health made audible'. Acknowledging with gratitude the good things that God is doing in your life is not only a sign of inner health but it is also the means for achieving inner health. As we pray in the preface of the Mass: 'You have no need of our praise, yet our desire to thank you is itself your gift.' God gives us the desire to acknowledge and praise him because in this way he makes us whole. When you are feeling peace and joy it can be easy to praise God. But even when you do not feel at peace with God it is still necessary to acknowledge his goodness and praise him. If the cause of the lack of peace is a deliberate sin then, of course, the first step in prayer is repentance. The great king David prayed:

> Have mercy on me, O God, in your goodness
> in your great tenderness wipe away my faults;
> wash me clean from my guilt
> purify me from my sin. (Ps. 51:1–2)

A confident appeal to God's goodness. Each time we sin we must turn to God, as king David did, and ask his forgiveness. We are in need of metanoia or repentance. In the New Rite of Penance we have this description of metanoia:

WE CAN ONLY APPROACH THE KINGDOM OF CHRIST BY metanoia. This is a profound change of the whole person by which we begin to consider, judge, and arrange our life according to the holiness and love of God, made manifest in his Son in the last days and given to us in abundance. The genuineness of the penance depends on this heartfelt contrition. For conversion should affect the whole person from within and toward a progressively deeper enlightenment and an ever-closer likeness to Christ.[7]

If our inability to acknowledge the good things that God is doing in our lives is caused by alienation from God, our union with God is restored through the grace of conversion. Conversion implies 'a profound change of the whole person'. In the words of Bishop Morris Maddocks conversion is 'a reorientation of the whole personality'.[8] The grace of conversion is the great work of God which we should acknowledge gratefully for the rest of our lives.

King David responded to the grace of conversion in his famous psalm for forgiveness. But he also asked for something else:

> Instil some joy and gladness into me,
> let the bones you have crushed rejoice again. (Ps. 51:8–9)

David knew the need for praise; he knew how important it was to acknowledge the goodness of God and God's goodness to himself. And, therefore, after confessing his sinfulness he asked for the gift of joy and gladness so that he could truly give glory to God. 'The glory of God', as St Irenaeus said 'is the human person fully alive.' As we acknowledge God's goodness to ourselves, as we thank him for all the good things he does in us, we give him glory because we become more fully alive in his presence. His name is hallowed in us.

Sometimes, however, you may experience great dryness in your prayer. You want to pray and feel unable; you want to acknowledge the great things that God is doing in you and you are unable to identify any of them; you long for the presence of God but you are only aware of his absence. In those times the only safe rule, given by all the great masters of the spiritual life, is to persevere in your time of prayer and wait for the Lord. The Holy Spirit teaches us to pray in this way:

> I waited and waited for Yahweh,
> now at last he has stooped to me
> and heard my cry for help.

> He pulled me out of the horrible pit,
> out of the slough of the marsh,
> has settled my feet on a rock
> and steadied my steps.

He has put a new song in my mouth,
a song of praise to our God; (Ps. 40:1-3)

Waiting on the Lord, especially in times of darkness or pain
or loss is the essential disposition of the disciple. Sr Bernarde
describes this spiritual condition well when she writes:

> YET, FOR ME NOW, I HAVE TO SAY, THAT THE TIMES THAT
> have been the richest and most growth filled in my life
> were the times I have experienced the cross of darkness,
> abandonment and loss. This is where, above all, I discovered
> the truth of who I am and who God was for me. It is from
> this place of acute pain of a recent bereavement (a close
> friend for forty years) that I share my thought with you
> now. In the past weeks in moments of poignant suffering
> and desolation the Word of God ministered powerfully to
> me through sometimes very mundane circumstances. God
> spoke directly and personally through a 'Prayer for the Day',
> a liturgical reading, a scripture quote on a card – words
> dropping like dew on arid ground bringing meaningful
> insights.

Sr Bernarde concludes her reflection on trying to pray in this
arid state by saying 'I have learned in the past few weeks the
truth of the words "blessed are they who mourn for they shall
be comforted", comforted with the knowledge that they are
growing creatively towards still more new life to become a new
creation.'

In times of dryness, when God seems far away, we wait for
the Lord. He will certainly come. Did you ever have the experience of waiting for a friend to turn up. A five minute wait is
bearable; an hour's wait can be very trying; a five hour's wait
could be quite unbearable. Yet, if you knew your friend was
really on the way you would wait, even if you had to wait all
day. In the same spirit we have to wait for the Lord. We have
his own assurance: 'That he will come is as certain as the
dawn' (Isa. 6:3). As we wait we should wait in a spirit of
acknowledging what the Lord is doing in our life. When he

comes we will be filled with the spirit of praise and thanks-giving.

Having acknowledged the good things which God is doing in our own life we should then acknowledge what he is doing in the lives of those who are close to us, especially in the lives of our enemies. This acknowledgement keeps us free from the danger of entering into judgement on our enemy. As we relate in prayer to our enemy we observe the command: 'Do not judge and you will not be judged; because the judgements you give are the judgements you will get' (Matt. 7:1). Acknowledging the good things that God is doing in the enemy keeps your spirit free from judgements.

ALLOWANCE

The third step in using the word of God in our prayer is to make allowance for our own weakness and sinfulness. The only thing we can do when we sin is to ask God's pardon. We accept his forgiveness with gratitude. Then we forgive ourselves. We cannot forgive our sins, but we must forgive ourselves for sinning. If we do not forgive ourselves we become burdened with guilt. And guilt becomes a very effective screen between the gracious presence of God and ourselves. You may have said of somebody, 'he feels so guilty that he can't look me in the eye.' Guilt prevents us from looking God in the eye too. There are, of course, two kinds of guilt. When we do wrong we experience 'guilt feelings'. That is good guilt. The Holy Spirit convicts us of our sin and invites us to turn to God for forgiveness. If, after we have turned contritely to the Lord, confessed our sins and received forgiveness, we still feel burdened with guilt that would be 'bad guilt'. It would, in effect, be a denial of God's promise of forgiveness:

Come now, let us talk this over,
says Yahweh.
Though your sins are like scarlet,
they shall be white as snow;

> though they are red as crimson,
> they shall be like wool. (Isa. 1:18)

Feeling guilty, after receiving the Lord's forgiveness, inhibits the heart to heart conversation with the Lord which is prayer. One good way to deal with such guilt feelings is to accept the approach of St Bernard:

> WHAT I CAN'T OBTAIN BY MYSELF, I APPROPRIATE TO MYSELF with confidence from the pierced side of the Lord because he is full of mercy. The mercy of God is, therefore, my merit. And what about my righteousness? O Lord, I shall remember only your righteousness. It is also mine because you are God's righteousness for me.[9]

When we confess our sins and ask God's pardon, Christ himself becomes our righteousness and our merit. We can, therefore, forgive ourselves and let go of our sins.

In the presence of God, then, we make allowance for our own weakness. Then we make allowance for the weakness of others, especially for the weakness of our enemy. We forgive the enemy just as we forgive ourselves. This is living by divine wisdom. God in his wisdom forgives us. We imitate his divine wisdom when we forgive others and make allowance for their sins against us. The most liberating thing we can say to God about our enemy, after we say that we forgive him, is that we make allowance for all his weaknesses: 'Father, forgive them, they don't know what they are doing.'

Faith sharing

1. What were your feelings when you first prayed the words 'I thank you for the wonder of myself'?
2. Now that you are living by the word of God and praising God for yourself, how do you feel?
3. Do you agree that 'self-acceptance' is the root of all things?

Scripture reading

The Vatican Council says: 'Such is the force and the power of the Word of God that it can serve the Church as her support and vigour, and the children of the Church as strength for their faith, food for the soul, and a pure and lasting fount of spiritual life.'[10] In the word of God you have everything you need for your spiritual life.

Sunday	Luke 12—13
Monday	Luke 14—15
Tuesday	Luke 16—18
Wednesday	Luke 19—20
Thursday	Luke 21—22
Friday	Luke 23—24
Saturday	John 1

5

Living by the word of promise

Pope John XXIII once asked a group of priests in Rome to explain to him the real reason for devotion to Our Blessed Lady. They produced many good theological reasons based on Scripture and the tradition of the Church. In the end the pope said: 'it is really very simple. We sum it all up in the words of the traditional invocation to Our Lady: "pray for us O holy Mother of God that we may be made worthy of the promises of Christ." '

The promises of Christ to the Church like the promises of God to his people in the Old Testament are at the very heart of the life of faith. A promise keeps us focused on the future. If parents promise their children on Monday to take them to the zoo on Saturday the children begin to live in great expectation: they cannot wait for Saturday. The visit to the zoo begins to give a whole new meaning to the week. That is the power of a promise.

It is not only children who respond to the power of the promise with hope and expectation. Adults need something to hope for also. The great Jewish psychiatrist, Viktor Frankl, discovered the need for hope in the future when he was a prisoner in death camps during the Second World War. He began to observe that prisoners who had something to live for had a much better chance of survival than those who had given up hope. Later on he wrote:

To quote Albert Einstein,

'THE MAN WHO REGARDS HIS LIFE AS MEANINGLESS IS NOT merely unhappy but hardly fit for life'. This is not only a matter of success and happiness, but also of survival. In the terminology of modern psychology, the will to meaning has 'survival value'. This was the lesson I had to learn in three years spent in Auschwitz and Dachau: other things being equal, those most apt to survive the camps were those orientated toward the future – toward a task, or a person, waiting for them in the future, toward a meaning to be fulfilled by them in the future.[1]

Frankl observed how frequently very strong men, who had given up hope, suddenly collapsed and died, while weak, sickly men, fired with hope, survived the horrors of the camps. This led him to develop a whole new approach to helping people which he called logotherapy. He explains this term: 'A literal translation of the term "logotherapy" is therapy through meaning.' Give a person a meaning for life, orient the person toward the future, and he will begin to live at his fullest potential. That is the power of a promise. A promise calls us into the future where the promise will be fulfilled.

In our own day Nelson Mandela witnesses to the same power of hope in the future. He was a political prisoner for twenty six years. He writes:

THE CHALLENGE FOR EVERY PRISONER, PARTICULARLY EVERY political prisoner, is how to survive prison intact, how to emerge from prison undiminished, how to conserve and even replenish one's beliefs . . . Prison and the authorities conspire to rob each man of his dignity. In and of itself, that assured that I would survive, for any man or institution that tries to rob me of my dignity will lose because I will not part with it at any price or under any pressure. I never seriously considered the possibility that I would not emerge from prison one day. I never thought that a life sentence truly meant life and that I would die behind bars. Perhaps I was denying this prospect because it was too unpleasant to contemplate. But I always knew that someday I would once again feel the grass under my feet and walk in the sunshine as a free man.[2]

Mandela was a future-orientated man. He lived for the promise of freedom. Three years after his release he was installed as the first black president of South Africa, and the racist Apartheid regime, which had imprisoned him, was dismantled. The promise of the future filled men like Nelson Mandela and Viktor Frankl, in every age, with the will to live and the determination to survive. God knows the power of a promise.

Living by the word of promise in the Old Testament

When our first parents were expelled from the garden of Eden God did not leave them without hope. He gave them this promise: the offspring of the woman would crush the head of the devil who had tempted her. God said to the serpent:

> I will make you enemies of each other;
> you and the woman,
> your offspring and her offspring.
> It will crush your head
> and you will strike at its heel. (Gen. 3:14–15)

The whole of the Bible can be read as the story of the fulfilment of that promise. The story begins to take on a concrete, historical form with the call of Abraham. In the Roman canon of the Mass we refer to Abraham as 'our father in faith'. How did he come to receive such a title? To answer this question let us reflect again on how God called Abraham: 'Yahweh said to Abram, Leave your country, your family and your father's house, for the land that I will show you. I will make you a great nation; I will bless you and make your name so famous that it will be used as a blessing' (Gen. 12:1–2). Abram did as the Lord asked him to do: he left his homeland, because of the promise of the Lord, and became a wanderer. After years of wandering Abram said to the Lord: 'My Lord Yahweh, what do you intend to give me? I go childless' (Gen. 15:2). God had promised to make him the father of a great nation and, as yet, he has no family of his own. He is living by the promise. After some more years of wandering God comes to Abraham again and makes a specific promise:

> AS FOR SARAI YOUR WIFE, YOU SHALL NOT CALL HER SARAI but Sarah. I will bless her and moreover give you a son by her. I will bless her and nations shall come out of her; kings of peoples shall descend from her. Abraham bowed to the ground, and laughed, thinking to himself 'Is a child to be born to a man one hundred years old, and will Sarah have a child at the age of ninety? (Gen. 17:15-17)

Despite his laughter God promised Abraham: 'your wife Sarah shall bear you a son whom you are to name Isaac. With him I will establish my Covenant, a Covenant in perpetuity, to be his God and the God of his descendants after him' (Gen. 17:19). This is the word of God's life giving promise. Abraham, despite all obstacles, lived by that word. Through Isaac and his descendants he did indeed become the father of a great nation, of God's people. That is why we call Abraham our 'father in faith'. The Vatican Council said:

> THE CHURCH OF CHRIST ACKNOWLEDGES THAT IN GOD'S plan of salvation the beginning of her faith and election is to be found in the patriarchs, Moses and the prophets. She professes that all Christ's faithful, who as men and women of faith are sons and daughters of Abraham (cf. Gal. 3:7), are included in the same patriarch's call and that the salvation of the Church is mystically prefigured in the exodus of God's chosen people from the land of bondage.[3]

(For the full story of Abraham read chapters 12 to 25 of Genesis).

Word of promise to Moses

The word of promise given to Abraham was given, centuries later, to Moses. By then the descendants of Isaac had indeed become a great nation. But they were slaves in Egypt. God appeared to Moses in 'The burning bush' and said to him, 'I am the God of your father, the God of Abraham, the God of Isaac and the God of Jacob' (Exod. 3:6). God told Moses that he saw the plight of his people in Egypt and that he was sending him to Pharaoh 'to bring my people out of Egypt'. Pharaoh was a cruel tyrant who was intent on killing Moses. We can, therefore, empathise with Moses when he said to God: 'Who am I to go to Pharaoh to bring the sons of Israel out of Egypt?' In response God gives Moses his reassuring word of promise: 'I shall be with you' (Exod. 3:12). Empowered by that word of promise Moses became the liberator of God's people. He led the people of Abraham, now known as the Israelites, out of Egypt, through the Red Sea, and into freedom because he knew God was with him.

This liberation of the people from slavery in Egypt, by the hand of God through Moses, was the defining moment in the history of God's people. They believed they were God's chosen people. God explained his choice of them in these words:

IF YAHWEH SET HIS HEART ON YOU AND CHOSE YOU, IT WAS not because you outnumbered other peoples; you were the least of all peoples. It was for love of you and to keep the oath he swore to your fathers that Yahweh brought you out with his mighty hand and redeemed you from the house of slavery, from the power of Pharaoh king of Egypt. Know then that Yahweh your God is God indeed, the faithful God who is true to his covenant and his graciousness for a thousand generations towards those who love him and keep his commandments, but who punishes in their own person those that hate him. (Deut. 7:7–8)

God is faithful to his promise; he expects his people to live in the expectation of the fulfilment of his promise.

The promise of the new covenant

The covenant which God entered into with his people, after he liberated them from Egypt was carved on stone. It was an external, written law. The new covenant, which he promised, would be written on their hearts. This is how the prophet Jeremiah foretells the new covenant:

SEE, THE DAYS ARE COMING – IT IS YAHWEH WHO SPEAKS – when I will make a new covenant with the House of Israel (and the House of Judah), but not a covenant like the one I made with their ancestors on the day I took them by the hand to bring them out of the land of Egypt ... No, this is the covenant I will make ... Deep within them I will plant my Law, writing it on their hearts. Then I will be their God and they shall be my people. There will be no further need for neighbour to try to teach neighbour, or brother to say to brother, 'Learn to know Yahweh!' No, they will all know me, the least no less than the greatest – it is Yahweh who speaks – since I will forgive their iniquity and never call their sins to mind. (Jer. 31:31–33)

The promise of a new covenant, a new law, an interior law written on the heart; the promise of a personal knowledge of God and the forgiveness of all our sins. St Augustine wrote: 'what else is it (the law written in our hearts) except the very presence of the Holy Spirit?' The great Scripture scholar Stanislaus Lyonnet, commenting on the new law written on the heart, wrote: 'The law of the Spirit is radically different by its very nature. It is not just a code, not even one "given by the Holy Spirit", but a law "produced in us by the Spirit", not a simple norm of action outside us but something that no legal legal code as such can possibly be: a new inner source of spiritual energy.'[4]

The promise of the new covenant brings:

- the hope of new spiritual energy

- the assurance of a personal knowledge of God
- the assurance of forgiveness of all sin

Pause for a moment and ask the Lord to fulfill his promise afresh in your life. Say, 'Lord, deep within me you have planted your law, writing it on my heart. Let me know the presence of your life-giving law.'

This hope of the new covenant will, of course, be fulfilled when Jesus takes the cup at the last supper and says, 'this is the cup of my blood of the new and everlasting covenant'. We will have that new source of spiritual energy when Christ pours out the Spirit. As he promised: 'you will receive power when the Holy Spirit comes.' We will consider this in detail in chapters 8 and 9.

The promises of Christ

Christ has made many and wonderful promises to us. They are not empty promises. Each promise will be fulfilled.

PROMISE OF REST

Jesus says: 'Come to me, all you who labour and are over burdened, and I will give you rest. Shoulder my yoke and learn from me, for I am gentle and humble in heart, and you will find rest for your souls. Yes, my yoke is easy and my burden light' (Matt. 11:28–30).

Jesus is faithful to his promise. He takes our burden and gives us rest. In the sacrament of the sick the Church prays for the sick: 'When they are afraid give them courage, when afflicted, give them patience, when dejected, afford them hope, and when alone, assure them of the support of your holy people.' The burden may be fear or affliction; it may be dejection or loneliness; it may be the experience of divorce and the break up of the family; unemployment or social deprivation may be the burden; indeed the burden can often be the Church's law which excludes those who married again after divorce from the sacraments. Whatever the burden we bring it to Christ with great confidence. He substitutes his rest for our burden. The promised rest for our souls comes when we seek to be like Christ, gentle and humble in heart. The proud heart cannot know the rest of Christ, nor can the aggressive spirit.

We live by this word of promise when we:

- come to Jesus with our burden
- learn from Jesus the meaning of gentleness of spirit
- lay our burden confidently at the feet of Jesus

When we find ourselves with Jesus he assures us: 'No one can come to me unless he is drawn by the Father who sent me, and I will raise him up on the last day' (John 6:44). It is the Father who draws us to Christ. Because our Father wants us to have rest for our souls he draws us to Jesus, the source of this rest. And Jesus says 'All that the Father gives me will come to me, and whoever comes to me, I shall not turn him away' (John 6:37). Because the Father is drawing us we should go with great confidence to Jesus. We have his assurance of acceptance.

Take a few moments in prayer now to do that. Identify your burden; bring it to the Lord; ask the Lord to teach you his own gentleness and humility; thank the Father for drawing you to Jesus and then wait for his promised rest and peace.

PROMISE OF THE SPIRIT

St Peter, in answer to Christ's question 'who do men say I am?' said, 'you are the Christ the Son of the living God.' From that time, St Matthew tells us, Jesus began to 'make it clear to his disciples that he was destined to go to Jerusalem and suffer grievously at the hands of the elders and chief priests and scribes, to be put to death and to be raised up on the third day' (Matt. 16:21). The shock this news caused the disciples is well illustrated by Peter's reaction. He had just confessed that Jesus is the Son of the living God. Yet, when he heard this disturbing, perplexing news of the Lord's approaching passion, Peter, we are told, 'taking him aside started to remonstrate with him. "Heaven preserve you, Lord;" he said, "this must not happen to you" ' (Matt. 16:22). We can imagine the dismay of the disciples. They had placed all their hopes in Christ. They believed in the Kingdom he was proclaiming. They had left all for the sake of the Kingdom. And now, before the Kingdom has been inaugurated, he tells them that he has to leave them through death. This is how St John describes this announcement:

'I did not tell you this from the outset,
because I was with you;
but now I am going to the one who sent me.
Not one of you has asked "where are you going?"
Yet you are sad at heart because I have told you this.'
    (John 16:5–6)

'Sad at heart' sums up how the disciples were feeling.

Knowing their sadness Jesus said something which must have, at the time, confused them even more:

'I must tell you the truth;
it is for your own good that I am going
because unless I go,
the Advocate will not come to you;
but if I go,
I will send him to you'. (John 16:6–7)

What did the disciples make of that? They surely must have said to themselves 'what could be better for us than to have the Lord with us always?' They saw his great miracles; they were enlightened and strengthened by his teaching; they were excited about the Kingdom which he was proclaiming and in which they wanted to play their part; they were constantly encouraged by his love and friendship. Yet the Lord is saying to them that it is better for them to have none of these things and to have the Holy Spirit, the Advocate. In Jesus' mind the invisible presence of the Holy Spirit is better for his disciples than his own visible presence. The disciples, of course, will not be able to understand this until after the resurrection.

Jesus not only promised them the Advocate but he also promised that they would know him:

'If you love me you will keep my commandments.
I shall ask the Father,
and he will give you another Advocate
to be with you for ever,
that Spirit of truth
whom the world can never receive
since it neither sees nor knows him;
but you know him,
because he is with you, he is in you. (John 14:15–17)

Christ's very specific promise is that we will know the Spirit.
We should ask the Lord to fulfill that promise each day. Whatever our situation, whatever the problems in our lives, we can
pray:

Father pour out your Spirit on my family (community
  or parish)
and grant us a new vision of your glory,
a new experience of your power,
a new consecration to your service,
that your love may grow among us and your Kingdom
  come.

When we get that new vision, experience that new power,
receive that new consecration we are getting to know the Spirit.
We get to know the Spirit through what he does in our lives.
In the Mass, for instance, we pray: 'May all of us who share
in the body and blood of Christ be brought together in unity
by the Holy Spirit.' The Spirit is the source of unity: unity in
our family, in our Church, in our world. When we have the
experience of being truly one with those we love we know
the presence of the Spirit. In the sacrament of reconciliation the
priest prays: 'God the Father of mercy has reconciled the whole
world to himself, through the death and resurrection of his Son
Jesus and he has sent the Holy Spirit among us for the forgiveness of our sins.' When we experience the forgiveness of sins
we are getting to know the Spirit.
  We live by this word of promise: 'you will know the

Spirit because he is with you he is in you.' That is the newness, the freshness of our Christian lives. Origen wrote in the third century: 'Do not think that the renewal of life that came about once and for all at the beginning is enough; it is necessary to continually renew the newness every day.'[5]

THE PROMISE OF
CHRIST'S ABIDING PRESENCE

In the Gospel according to Matthew there is no specific account of Pentecost. Jesus leaves the disciples with these words: 'Know that I am with you always; yes, to the end of time' (Matt. 28:20). Christ promises to be with us always. This is the promise which has strengthened countless Christians in the face of all kinds of dangers throughout the centuries. Reflecting on why the Gospel according to Matthew does not have an account of Jesus giving the Spirit to his disciples, George Montague writes:

THE REASON APPEARS TO BE THAT MATTHEW CONSIDERS THE resurrection and glorification of Jesus to be his entering, not heaven, but the church as an abiding presence. He is the promised Immanuel (Isa. 23) whose final words to the church are: 'I am with you all days, even to the consummation of the world' (28:20). That means, though, that the Spirit which the Father places upon Jesus (3:11; 12:28) rests upon the church which is one with him. The church has the Spirit, then, not because Jesus left the Spirit as his replacement until he returns (the view of Luke and John) or because at some moment during his ministry or after the resurrection he specifically conveyed the Spirit of the church, but rather because, remaining with the church, Jesus baptises with the Spirit through sharing his own baptism with the disciples of all ages. Jesus does not give the Spirit to the church but rather receives it for the church. Whence the intimate and necessary identification of Christian baptism with his.[6]

Christ is with us. That is the life-giving promise we must hold on to. In your situation right now Jesus says: 'know, I am with you.' When Moses had to face a difficult task he said to God 'Who am I to go to Pharaoh to bring the sons of Israel out of Egypt?' and God responded: 'I shall be with you.' In the same way, Jesus says to each of us, when we are faced with difficult situations or decisions, 'I am with you always.' When you have to make a difficult decision turn to Jesus and say, 'let's make this decision together, Lord.' Because we are men and women of the promise we always live in hope.

Faith sharing

1. Which of the promises of God do you live by most?
2. How do you cope when you feel that the promise has not been fulfilled?
3. How do you bring the word of promise into your daily life?

Scripture reading

'The word of God is something alive and active: it cuts like any double-edged sword but more finely; it can slip through the place where soul is divided from the spirit, or joints from the marrow; it can judge the secret emotions and thoughts' (Heb. 4:12–13). As you read the Scriptures this week become aware that you are hearing the living word of God.

Sunday	John 2—3
Monday	John 4—5
Tuesday	John 6
Wednesday	John 7
Thursday	John 8
Friday	John 9—10
Saturday	John 11—12

6

Abba, Father

A missionary sister writes from Ecuador:

LIKE MANY PEOPLE OF MY GENERATION – NEARING 60 –
I grew up with a stern father, and an image of God the
Father as very strict – demanding perfection from me all
the time, with that infamous 'big book' ready to jot down
my failures. Obviously I failed in my religious life. Nobody
could live up to what I thought was expected of me. So I
left, and tried to find happiness in possessions and addictions. God my Father waited patiently, lovingly and through
many failures and mistakes, he drew me back to himself.
During a retreat before coming out here the true image of
God my loving father was revealed to me and I'm still discovering the wonders of his goodness. I am now working in
a slum area of Ecuador trying to help his poor children. I
brought back a plaque from Kinnoull:[1] 'I will never forget
you, I, I have carved you on the palm of my hands', and it
hangs on my wall as a constant reminder. The one phrase I
carried away from Kinnoull (thanks to Fr Charlie) is that
I am precious in his eyes.

When this sister's image of God was that of a stern father,
demanding perfection at every turn, she did not have the
strength to live her life as a religious. When, however, as she
says 'the true image of God my loving Father was revealed to
me', she has the strength to work for the poor in a slum in
Ecuador. She sought happiness in 'possessions and addictions'.
Now she finds fulfilment in doing the Father's will in serving
the poor.

Jesus came to change our 'image of God'. Who is God? What

do we know about him? Can we ever know him? It is good to remind ourselves that God in himself is total mystery, total silence, and we would have known very little about God if he had not broken the silence. That is what we mean by revelation: God breaking the silence about himself. And God breaks the silence about himself in the same way as we break the silence about ourselves. God spoke. As Scripture says: 'At various times in the past and in various different ways, God spoke to our ancestors through the prophets; but in our own times, the last days, he has spoken to us through his Son, the Son that he has appointed to inherit everything and through whom he has made everything there is' (Heb. 1:1–2).

We would have known very little about God if God had not spoken. 'The desire for God', as the *Catechism of the Catholic Church* says, 'is written in the human heart because man is created for God and by God.'[2] Because of this desire the human heart is always searching. As St Augustine put it: 'You have made us for yourself, O Lord, and our hearts will find no rest until they rest in you.' The Church has always taught that we can come to acknowledge of the existence of God by observing the world which exists. St Paul said: 'For what can be known about God is perfectly plain to them since God himself has made it plain. Ever since God created the world his everlasting power and deity – however invisible – have been there for the mind to see in the things he has made' (Rom. 1:19–20). The human heart's desire for God has led people, in every age, to search for God. Indeed the *Catechism* says:

IN MANY WAYS, THROUGHOUT HISTORY DOWN TO THE present day, men have given expression to their quest for God in their religious beliefs and behaviour: in prayers, sacrifices, rituals, meditations and so forth. These forms of religious expression, despite the ambiguities they often bring with them, are so universal that one may well call man a religious being.[3]

God does not leave us, however, to the power of our own intellects. He wants to make himself known to us. That personal knowledge of God is promised in the new covenant: 'they will all know me, the least no less than the greatest' (Jer. 31:34). Jesus sums up his work in terms of making God's name known:

I HAVE MADE YOUR NAME KNOWN TO THE MEN YOU TOOK from the world to give to me. They were yours and you gave them to me, and they have kept your word. Now at last they know that all you have given me comes indeed from you; for I have given them the teaching you gave to me and they have truly accepted this, that I came from you, and have believed that it was you who sent me. (John 17:6–8)

When his disciples had accepted all this Jesus was able to say to the God: 'I have finished the work that you gave me to do' (John 17:4). Jesus sees his work on earth completed because he has revealed God's name to his disciples and they have accepted it. And the name that Jesus gave to God is Abba.

The Word incarnate

We can come to the knowledge of God's existence through the light of our own reason; we could never arrive at a knowledge of the intimate nature of God without a direct revelation from God. To communicate directly with us God had simultaneously to do two things: he had to speak a word which we human beings could understand and he had to speak a word which, at the same time, would truly manifest his own inner being. God had that word to speak. As the Scripture says:

In the beginning was the Word,
the Word was with God
and the Word was God. (John 1:1)

Because the Word was God, the Word could clearly and adequately speak about the inner being of God. But if the Word spoke a divine word we would not be able to understand it. Our human limitations required that somehow that divine Word was spoken to us as a human word. How could the infinite Word of God be spoken as a human word? St John tells us:

> The Word was made flesh,
> he lived among us,
> and we saw his glory,
> the glory that is his as the only Son of the Father,
> full of grace and truth. (John 1:14)

The infinite Word of God becomes flesh. Jesus, the Word incarnate, speaks that infinite Word to us in our own human words. And Jesus says to us, 'the one I call my Father is also your Father.' That is what we mean by revelation. God in his own inner nature is total silence. In breaking the silence, through the Word made flesh, we receive the knowledge that God, the source of all power, the maker of heaven and earth, does not want to be known by his omnipotence, his infinitude, his absolute perfection. God wants to be known by a name which is in the heart of every child: the name 'Father'.

In teaching us to pray Jesus did not tell us to say almighty, everlasting, eternal and infinite divine One. He told us to say 'Abba, Father'. It was as if Jesus said: 'if you want to come to God you must come with the sentiment of a child in your heart and the word of a child on your lips.' God is our infinite creator. But the word which best describes the relationship that he has with us is 'Father'. When Jesus said to his Father, 'I have made your name known to the men you took from the word and gave to me' (John 17:6), he was saying that he had revealed to them the innermost nature of God. 'A name expresses a person's essence and identity and the meaning of the person's life. God has a name; he is not an anonymous force. To disclose one's name is to make oneself known to others; in a way it is to hand oneself over by becoming accessible, capable of being known more intimately and addressed personally.'[4] Jesus makes God totally accessible to us by teaching us to address God, the creator of all, as Abba, loving Father. He opens up to us the possibility of getting to know God in an entirely new way – in an intimate, personal, loving way.

The image of 'father' expresses the loving care and goodness of God. Could we also use the image of 'mother' to speak about God? The *Catechism of the Catholic Church* states: 'By calling God "Father", the language of faith indicates two things: that God is first origin of everything and transcendent authority; and that he is at the same time goodness and loving care for all his children. God's parental tenderness can also be expressed by the image of motherhood, which emphasises God's immanence, the intimacy between Creator and creature.'[5] That is official teaching in the Church today. If the image of 'father' doesn't speak to you about the goodness and love of God you should use the image of 'mother'. God compares himself to a mother:

> At her breast will her nurselings be carried
> and fondled in her lap.
> Like a son comforted by his mother
> will I comfort you. (Isa. 66:13)

And in the psalms we read:

> Enough for me to keep my soul tranquil and quiet
> like a child in its mother's arm,
> as content as a child that has been weaned. (Ps. 131.2)

God calls us into an intimate, trusting, loving relationship with himself. This relationship expresses itself, not only in our prayer, but most of all in the way we begin to depend on God for all good things.

Proof of sonship

In the Mass as we prepare for the Lord's prayer, we say: 'Jesus has taught us to call God our Father and so we have the courage to say, Our Father . . .' We can call God Father because he has given us the greatest proof he could that we are his children. St Paul says: 'The proof that you are sons is that God has sent the Spirit of his Son into our hearts: the Spirit that cries "Abba, Father", and it is this that makes you a son, you are not a slave any more; and if God has made you son, then he has made you heir' (Gal. 4:6). In his letter to the Romans, St Paul says that 'The Spirit himself and our spirit bear united witness that we are the children of God' (Rom. 8:16). It is not just the teaching of Jesus which enables us to say 'Father'; it is the Spirit of Jesus within our spirit and united to our spirit who makes us truly sons and daughters of the Father. Through the transforming action of the Spirit we are made one with Christ, divinised. As we pray in the Mass, 'By the mystery of this water and wine may we come to share in the divinity of Christ, who humbled himself to share in our humanity.' This divinisation takes place through the sanctifying and transforming presence of the Holy Spirit. Writing in the fifth century, St Gregory Nazianzen said: 'Acknowledge that you have been made a son of God, a co-heir with Christ. Acknowledge, and now I speak with daring, that you have been made divine. From where and from whom have all these benefits come to you?'[6] Having transformed us into the children of God the Spirit then teaches us how to pray. He cries out 'Abba, Father'. That is our new relationship with God. St Ignatius of Antioch, one of the great early martyrs wrote: 'I feel a spring of living water within me murmuring: come to the Father.'[7]

This revelation that the almighty God, the creator of all things, is our loving Father transforms our attitudes and our approach to God in prayer. Our first parents, after their sin, lost confidence in the abiding, fatherly love of God: 'The man and his wife heard the sound of Yahweh God walking in the garden in the cool of the day, and they hid from Yahweh God among the trees of the garden' (Gen. 3:8). Fear and distrust had entered their lives. Their vision of God had changed. Ever since then God has been trying to convince the human race that he loves us, that he is on our side, that he wants to save us from our sins and unite us to himself for ever. Jesus called this desire in the heart of God 'the Gospel', the good news of God's intentions toward us. And Jesus told us to acknowledge all this by one simple word: Abba. That says it all. When we address God as Abba we not only profess our faith in the

Gospel preached by Jesus, we also acknowledge that through his death and resurrection we have become children of God. As St John said, 'Think of the love that the Father has lavished on us, by letting us be called God's children' and that is what we are' (1 John 3:1).

Our whole relationship, then, with God is deeply personal and intimate. The reaction of children at the sight of their father teaches us how to pray. As soon as children see their father returning from work they run to meet him. So often we treat God as if he were a stranger, as if we did not really know him. Jesus said: 'Everything has been entrusted to me by my Father; and no one knows the Son except the Father, just as no one knows the Father except the Son and those to whom the Son chooses to reveal him' (Matt. 11:27).

Pause for a moment now and ask Jesus to reveal the Father to you. Listen to the voice of the Spirit within crying 'Abba, Father'.

Angela's testimony

The following testimony expresses in terms of a woman's own experience of God her Father much of what I am trying to say in this chapter:

ALTHOUGH I KNEW THAT MY FATHER LOVED ME VERY MUCH, circumstances, being as they were, I was not able to experience that love.

Even as a tiny child I had a strong sense of God, and a close relationship with Jesus, but I never knew God as my Father, or had any personal relationship with him.

Then, one day, Jesus took me to his Father. I was at a large gathering of people singing hymns of praise and worship. Suddenly I felt myself to be in the presence of God in a very intimate way. I knew him to be my Father, and I his child, and that he loved me dearly. I put my arms around him, asking him with all my heart, that my life would be pleasing to him, and that I would fulfill his plan for me.

Since that day, I have known God as a tender and loving Father. He cares about the little details of my life, and I am aware of his provision and protection in very ordinary circumstances.

Sometimes I experience myself in his arms, and there is a security I have never known before. I understand now the meaning of a Father's love, a tender forgiving love, and that He has hopes and plans for my life (as a human father would).

I come to him often as a Father, and speak to him about myself and others. He always listens and understands, and prayers are answered in many unexpected ways.

Sometimes I feel the tender love he has for his children, and the longing of his heart that all may know him as their Father.

I pray that my life will give him glory and honour and that I will bring others to know him.

Angela's testimony highlights two important facts:

1. Jesus brought her to the Father. Jesus himself said: 'No one can come to the Father except through me' (John 14:6).

2. In her first personal experience of God as her loving Father she asked, 'with all my heart that my life might be pleasing to him'. She said, in effect, 'hallowed be thy name'. Her prayer is that 'my life will give him glory and honour'.

The fact that Angela's first response to her 'experience of the Father' was her heartfelt request that her whole life would be pleasing to him and that he would be glorified in her life is a good indicator that this was an authentic religious experience. This experience is still bearing fruit in her life. She has become an intercessor for all God's people. Only those who know the goodness, the kindness and the mercy of the Father can give themselves wholeheartedly to the prayer of intercession.

Faith sharing

1. What is your awareness of God as Father?
2. Are there elements in your image of God that make it difficult for you to relate to God as Father?
3. Have you experienced the Fatherhood/Motherhood of God in any way in your life, especially in your prayer during the week?

Scripture reading

'All scripture is inspired by God and can profitably be used for teaching, for refuting error, for guiding people's lives and teaching them to be holy. This is how the man dedicated to God becomes fully equipped and ready for any good work' (2 Tim. 3:16–17). By prayerfully reading the Scriptures each day you are preparing yourself for a life of good works.

Sunday	John 13—14
Monday	John 15—16
Tuesday	John 17—18
Wednesday	John 19—21
Thursday	Acts 1—2
Friday	Acts 3—4
Saturday	Acts 6—7

7

Jesus Christ is Lord

The first proclamation of our Christian faith found in the New Testament is enshrined in the words 'Jesus Christ is Lord'. This proclamation, like the assurance that we are sons and daughters of the Father, is the work of the Holy Spirit. St Paul tells us that 'no one can say "Jesus is Lord" unless he is under the influence of the Holy Spirit' (1 Cor. 12:1). St Peter, on the first Pentecost Sunday, proclaimed to the people of Jerusalem: 'For this reason the whole House of Israel can be certain that God has made this Jesus whom you crucified both Lord and Christ' (Acts 2:36).

Jesus Christ is Lord. We will consider each of these holy names. Fr Congar says that the Scholastic theologians, that is the great theologians of the Middle Ages whose thought has dominated Catholic theology for the past six hundred years, regarded 'Christ' simply as a proper noun or name that could be replaced equally well by 'Jesus' or 'the Lord'.[1] If theologians have confused the holy names in this way we should not be surprised if many people regard 'Christ' as a surname. They may speak of 'Jesus Christ' in the same way in which they would speak of 'John Smith'. But whereas in the case of John, 'Smith' is his family name, in the case of Jesus, 'Christ' is not his family name. We do not know the family name of the holy family. This should alert us to the fact that when we are considering the holy names of 'Jesus', of 'Christ' and of 'Lord' we are looking at names that hold great significance for our salvation, names that have been revealed to us by God.

For many years, I think, I used the names 'Jesus Christ' as if 'Christ' was a surname. I had not really thought about the meaning of the names. It was only when I began to reflect on the role of the Holy Spirit in the life of Jesus that I began to see that 'Christ' is not a surname and 'Lord' is not an honorary title. Jesus is Christ because of the work of the Spirit, just as Jesus is Lord because of the same Spirit. We will look at this in the three stages of the life of Mary's son, the Son of God on earth.

Jesus

God sent the angel Gabriel to Mary. He greeted her with these words: 'Rejoice so highly favoured! The Lord is with you.' This formula 'the Lord is with you' is used frequently in the Old Testament and 'it is often connected with an action that has to be done according to God's plan and is connected with the presence of the Spirit in the one who has to perform this action'.[2] Then the angel said to Mary: 'Listen! You are to conceive a son and you must name him Jesus. He will be great and will be called the Son of the Most High' (Luke 1:32). In the Hebrew language the word 'Jesus' means 'God saves'. When the angel spoke to St Joseph in a dream he said: 'Joseph son of David, do not be afraid to take Mary home as your wife, because she has conceived what is in her by the Holy Spirit. She will give birth to a son and you must name him Jesus, because he is the one who is to save his people from their sins' (Matt. 1:20–21). Every time in our prayer when we say 'Jesus' we are saying: 'you are the one who saves us from our sins.' God alone can forgive sins. When we recognise that Jesus saves us from our sins we are professing our faith in the divinity of Jesus, the Son of God made man. The *Catechism of the Catholic Church* puts it this way:

THE NAME 'JESUS' SIGNIFIES THAT THE VERY NAME OF GOD is present in the person of his Son, made man for the universal and definitive redemption from sins. It is the divine name that alone brings salvation, and henceforth all can invoke his name, for Jesus united himself to all men through his Incarnation, so that 'there is no other name under heaven given among men by which we must be saved'.[3]

St Paul discovered this for himself in a very dramatic way. He was persecuting the disciples of Jesus. He had set out for Damascus to arrest the followers of Jesus and bring them back to Jerusalem for punishment. Scripture explains what happened: 'Suddenly, while he was travelling to Damascus and just before he reached the city, there came a light from heaven all round him. He fell to the ground and then he heard a voice saying, "Saul, Saul, why are you persecuting me?" ' Saul knew that he was persecuting the followers of a dead man called Jesus, but who was this man speaking to him from the light? He asked, 'Who are you Lord?' The voice answered: 'I am Jesus and you are persecuting me' (Acts 9:3–6). Hearing the name 'Jesus' uttered from the light transformed Saul. He was converted and became the great St Paul. And the name of Jesus took on a whole new dimension for him as we can see from his letters:

> But God raised him high
> and gave him a name
> which is above all other names
> so that all beings
> in the heavens, on earth and in the underworld,
> should bend the knee at the name of Jesus
> and that every tongue should acclaim
> Jesus Christ is Lord,
> to the glory of God the Father. (Phil. 2:9–11)

Coming to believe in Jesus is always accompanied with great reverence for his holy name. It is by the name of Jesus that we are saved. St Peter told the Jews: 'For of all the names in the world given to men, this (the name of Jesus) is the only one by which we can be saved' (Acts 4:12). Jesus assures us of his saving presence: 'where two or three come together in my name, I shall be there with them' (Matt. 18:20). And because he is with us he promises: 'Whatever you ask for in my name I will do, so that the Father may be glorified in the Son. If you ask for anything in my name, I will do it' (John 14:13).

Reverence, awe, respect, love, gratitude, these are some of the emotions and attitudes which we have for the holy name of Jesus. We conclude all our prayers in the Mass with the formula: 'through our Lord Jesus Christ your Son'. The name of Jesus is at the centre of our prayer. When we say the Hail Mary we proclaim 'blessed is the fruit of thy womb, Jesus'. Just to repeat the name of Jesus in our heart is to pray in a most fruitful way. Some years ago I was in the Benedictine monastery at Pecos, where they teach great respect for the holy name. As members of the community were praying with me the only prayer they said was 'Jesus'. Repeating the holy name over and over again, with great reverence and devotion, they brought great peace into my heart. The great saints and mystics of the Eastern Church developed what is known as 'The Jesus prayer'. They taught their followers to repeat in their hearts the words: 'Lord Jesus Christ, Son of God, have mercy on me a sinner.' They discovered that by repeating this prayer with love and devotion it suddenly, as it were, leaves the head and becomes embedded in the heart and, when the head is busy about others things, the heart still repeats the prayer. Even if the only prayer we said in the whole day was the reverential utterance of the name of Jesus we would have prayed well.

Pause for a moment now and reflect on your reverence for the name of Jesus. Scripture says, 'at the name of Jesus every knee should bow'. Now repeat prayerfully the name of Jesus in your heart. Keep the holy name in your heart. Say just the name 'Jesus' or, if you prefer use the Jesus Prayer, 'Lord Jesus Christ, Son of God, have mercy on me, a sinner.'

Christ

Jesus was conceived through the power of the Holy Spirit. As we say in the Apostles' Creed: 'I believe in Jesus Christ his only Son, our Lord, who was conceived by the Holy Spirit and born of the virgin Mary.' The eternal Son of God became a human being like us. He was endowed with all our faculties: a human mind and heart, human emotions and intelligence, human hopes and desires. Jesus, by divine nature the Son of God, by human nature the Son of Mary, is forever totally identified with our sinful human history and destiny. He manifested that identification in a remarkable way when, in solidarity with all the people who were going to be baptised by John the Baptist, he went and asked for baptism at the hands of John. The Scripture says: 'John tried to dissuade him. "It is I who need baptism from you" he said "and yet you come to me!" But Jesus replied, "Leave it like this for the time being; it is fitting that we should, in this way, do all that righteousness demands." At this, John gave in to him' (Matt. 3:13–15). John's was a baptism for repentance. Jesus was sinless. He did not need repentance. Yet, because he saw in John's baptism the plan of God, he submitted to it. He said of those who accepted that baptism: 'All the people who heard him, and the tax collectors too, acknowledged God's plan by accepting baptism from John' (Luke 7:29).

St Luke tells us that after his baptism Jesus was at prayer. Whenever St Luke says Jesus was at prayer something very significant is about to happen. During his prayer, 'heaven opened and the Holy Spirit descended on him in bodily shape, like a dove. And a voice came from heaven, You are my Son, the Beloved; my favour rests on you' (Luke 3:22).

For many years I did not give much attention to this coming of the Holy Spirit on Jesus after his baptism. I think my attitude was something like this: Jesus is the eternal Son of God, one with the Father and one with the Holy Spirit. He had the Spirit even before he went to the Jordan. Therefore, this new manifestation of the Spirit must have been for the sake of the others. I was not, therefore, in a frame of mind to ponder the meaning of the word Christ. The word 'Christ' comes from the Greek translation of the Hebrew 'Messiah', which means 'anointed'. Christ means 'the anointed one'. (It is not a surname!) In the writings of the early Church Fathers the anointing of Jesus at the Jordan received great attention:

THESE THEOLOGIANS OF THE EARLIEST TIMES WERE NOT
unaware of the Holy Spirit's presence in Jesus from the
moment of his human birth; they did however attribute a
different and decisive significance to the solemn anointing
received by Jesus in the Jordan to mark the beginning of his
messianic mission. According to some of them, just as at the
incarnation, the Word had become 'Jesus', so at his baptis-
mal anointing he had become 'Christ', that is to say God's
anointed one, the Messiah. As they saw it, the mystery of
the anointing was so important that the very name 'Christians' was derived from it: 'This is why we are called
Christians (*christianoi*), writes one of them, 'because we are
anointed (*chriometha*) with the oil of God'. Christians
according to this explanation, did not so much mean 'followers of Christ', as the pagans at Antioch who had been
the first to call them this intended (cf. Acts 11:26), but rather
'sharers in Christ's anointing'.[4]

It would help us to focus our minds on the meaning of
'Christ' if instead of simply saying 'Jesus Christ' we said 'Jesus,
the anointed one'. St Basil wrote:

TO NAME CHRIST IS TO CONFESS THE WHOLE TRINITY,
because it indicates the God who anointed, and the Son who
was anointed, and that wherewith he was anointed, namely
the Spirit, as we learnt from Peter in Acts: Jesus of Nazareth,
whom God anointed with the Holy Spirit' (Acts 10:38). And
in Isaiah we read, 'The Spirit of the Lord is upon me, because
He has anointed me' (Isa. 61:1); and the Psalmist, 'Wherefore
God, even your God, has anointed you with the oil of
gladness'.[5]

The *Catechism* returns to this early understanding of the significance of the anointing of Christ: 'Jesus' messianic consecration reveals his divine mission, "for the name 'Christ' implies
'he who anointed', 'he who was anointed' and 'the very anointing with which he was anointed'. The one who anointed is the
Father, the one who was anointed is the Son, and he was

anointed with the Spirit who is the anointing." [6] At his baptism in the Jordan, therefore, we have what Pope John Paul called a trinitarian theophany.[7] The voice which is heard is the Father's, acknowledging Jesus as his 'beloved Son', and the anointing which Jesus receives is the anointing with the Holy Spirit. The Spirit descends and rests on Jesus.

Jesus receives the Holy Spirit for his mission; he also receives the Holy Spirit for us. St John says: 'Indeed, from his fullness we have all received, yes, grace in return for grace' (John 1:16). God the Father gave the fullness of the Spirit to Jesus and from that fullness we receive. As one ancient writer put it: 'the fountain head of the entire Holy Spirit abides in Christ, so that from him might be drawn streams of grace and wondrous deeds, because the Holy Spirit dwells affluently in Christ.'[8] Jesus shares with us the anointing which he himself received from the Holy Spirit. The Vatican Council said: 'The Lord Jesus "whom the Father consecrated and sent into this world" (John 10:36) makes his whole Mystical Body sharer in the anointing of the Spirit wherewith he has been anointed.'[9] We can say that the Church is the community of those who share in the anointing of the anointed one. The fullness of Jesus from which we share is the fullness of the Holy Spirit. Jesus cannot share with us the unique union with God whereby he and the Father are one. We call that union the 'hypostatic union' – unique to Jesus and incommunicable to us. He can communicate to us what he received from the Father, namely the anointing with the Holy Spirit through which he becomes 'the Christ', the Messiah, the anointed one. This truth is clearly expressed in the way we used to talk about baptism. I have often heard people, usually the older generation, ask 'when is the christening?' meaning when will the baby be baptised. It is lovely to hear parents say: 'we are going to have the baby christened.' That is a very profound and specific way of talking about the effects of baptism. The baby, in the language of St Paul, is baptised 'into Christ'. He or she comes to share in what makes Jesus 'the Christ', namely the anointing of the Holy Spirit. Through his christening the person becomes 'Christ-ed', he becomes 'a

Christ', an anointed one. When we ask people their 'Christian name' we are asking them: 'what name did you receive when you were joined to Christ, when you were "Christ-ed", when you became a Christ, an anointed one?' We received our name then because our christening was our rebirth. In our baptism we were 'born again of water and the Holy Spirit' and we became one with Christ. St Paul says: 'And for anyone who is in Christ, there is a new creation; the old creation is gone, and the new one is here. It is all God's work' (2 Cor. 5:17). Our Christian name is given to 'the new creation' which we became when we were christened, when we were joined to Christ and shared in the anointing of the Holy Spirit with which the Father anointed him. What does that anointing do in our life? In everyday life, in the humdrum of the ordinary what difference does our christening make? Guardini wrote:

THE PERSON HIMSELF IS CHANGED BY THIS DAILY CONTACT with Christ, becoming more and more similar to his model. The believer remains in his profession; he remains the same trader, postman, doctor that he was, with the same duties. The machine does not function better in his hand then in that of another; the diagnosis is not easier than it was, yet work performed in Christ is somehow different. No longer over-estimated, but properly evaluated, it assumes a new dignity and earnestness; is performed with a new conscientiousness. The same holds true for worries and pain and all other human need. The difference is indefinable, visible only in the result: here an illness or loss borne with quiet heroism, there an old enmity healed. In Christ all things are changed.[10]

Everything is changed when we live and work in Christ because Christ fills us with the anointing of the Spirit with which he himself was anointed.

Pause for a moment now; see the Holy Spirit coming on Jesus and anointing him; then see Jesus sharing that anointing with yourself. And with St Peter say to Jesus: 'You are the Christ, the Son of the living God.'

Devotion to Christ as the anointed one is beautifully expressed in the prayer which is called 'St Patrick's Breastplate':

Christ be with me, Christ within me,
Christ behind me, Christ before me,
Christ beside me, Christ to win me,
Christ to comfort and restore me,
Christ beneath me, Christ above me,
Christ in quiet, Christ in danger,
Christ in hearts of all that love me
Christ in mouth of friend and stranger.

All reflection on the name of Christ should lead us to surrender in trust and devotion to Jesus, the Messiah, the Son of the Living God.

Lord

In the Apostles' Creed we say: 'I believe in Jesus Christ his only Son, our Lord.' Our proclamation of faith is: Jesus Christ is Lord. The title Lord is not interchangeable with the title Christ, nor is it interchangeable with the name of Jesus. We are saying something very specific about Jesus when we say he is 'the Christ'. We are saying that God his Father has anointed him with the Holy Spirit. What are we saying when we profess that Jesus is the Lord? The Gospel puts it this way: 'Meanwhile the eleven disciples set out for Galilee, to the mountain where Jesus had arranged to meet them. When they saw him they fell down before him, though some hesitated. Jesus came up and spoke to them. He said, "All authority in heaven and on earth has been given to me"' (Matt. 28:16–17). God alone holds all authority in heaven and earth. Jesus is now saying that all that divine authority has been given to him. From heaven Jesus, in our humanity, now exercises that authority. St Mark paints this picture: 'And so the Lord Jesus, after he had spoken to them, was taken up into heaven; there at the right hand of God he took his place, while they, going out, preached everywhere, the

Lord working with them and confirming the word by the signs that accompanied it' (Mark 16:20).

The apostles had lived and worked with Jesus for about three years. They had got to know him very well during those years. They had listened to his teaching; they had observed his life of prayer and service; they saw the miracles he worked to heal the sick and cast out evil spirits; they were encouraged by his love and support and very proud that he called them his friends. But their world fell apart when he was arrested. One of them had betrayed him, another had denied him, and the rest of them fled. They were devastated by his cruel crucifixion. Yet, within a few days they were back together again proclaiming to the Jews, in the words of St Peter: 'For this reason the whole House of Israel can be certain that God had made this Jesus whom you crucified both Lord and Christ' (Acts 2:36). The cause of their devastation, the crucifixion of Jesus, became the central message of their proclamation: you crucified him, God has raised him up; you rejected him as a blasphemer and a sinner, God has made him 'both Lord and Christ'. As St Peter said to the chief priests and rulers of the people: 'This is the stone rejected by you the builders, but which has proved to be the keystone' (Acts 4:11). The disciples, whose faith and world had been shattered by the crucifixion, who had lost their master through death, now have a completely new relationship with him. He is not just their friend and master; nor is he just the great prophet, the Messiah promised through the prophets. He is something more. St Thomas, who doubted the story that he had risen from the dead, when he saw him with his own eyes, put it into words for them: 'My Lord and my God' (John 20:28). The man they had walked the roads of Galilee with, who got tired and exhausted, just as they did, who liked to eat and drink, just as they did, was all the time the Son of the living God. They knew, as the two disciples on the road to Emmaus said to the Risen Lord whom they did not recognise, that 'he proved he was a great prophet by the things he said and did in the sight of God and of the whole people'. And they expressed their own expectations at the time: 'Our own hope had been that he would be the one to set Israel free' (Luke 24:19–20). Jesus' resurrection introduced a whole new and totally unexpected dimension into their relationship with him: the dimension of faith.

Jesus underlined this new faith dimension in their relationship when he said to Thomas: 'You believe because you can see me, happy are those who have not seen and yet believe' (John 20:29). St Paul stressed this new faith way of knowing Christ: 'Even if we did once know Christ in the flesh, that is not how we know him now' (2 Cor. 5:17). We know him now through faith. After his resurrection and ascension we cannot know Christ in the flesh. We cannot see him with our physical eyes. We now know through faith that he is sitting at the right hand of the Father. The *Catechism of the Catholic Church* says:

> BEING SEATED AT THE FATHER'S RIGHT HAND SIGNIFIES THE inauguration of the Messiah's kingdom, the fulfilment of the prophet Daniel's vision concerning the Son of man: 'To him was given dominion and glory and kingdom, that all peoples, nations, and languages should serve him; his dominion is an everlasting dominion, which shall not pass away, and his kingdom one that shall not be destroyed' (Dan. 7:14). After this event the apostles became witnesses of the 'kingdom that will have no end.[11]

Having known Jesus in the flesh the disciples now know him in an entirely new way. Now they know the Lordship of Jesus. In the book of Revelation the language of the Lordship of Jesus takes a very colourful form. John had a vision of the Lord on the island of Patmos. He tells us: 'When I saw him, I fell down in a dead faint at his feet, but he touched me with his right hand and said, "Do not be afraid; it is I, the First and the Last; I am the Living One. I was dead and now I am to live for ever and ever, and I hold the keys of death and the underworld"' (Rev. 1:17). The Lord tells John to write to the 'angels' of the seven churches of Asia with a message. In each message his sovereignty is proclaimed:

HERE IS THE MESSAGE of the First and the Last, who was dead and has come to life again.

HERE IS THE MESSAGE of the Son of God who has eyes like a burning flame and feet like burnished bronze.

HERE IS THE MESSAGE of the one who holds the seven spirits of God and the seven stars'.

Here is the message of the holy and faithful one *who has the key of David, so that when he opens nobody can close, and when he closes nobody can open.* (Rev. 2 and 3)

With these powerful images Scripture makes it clear that Jesus, who had been crucified, now lives in the power and the glory of God. He is King of kings and Lord of lords. Faith in the divinity of Jesus, in his Lordship, forced the disciples to rethink not only their personal relationship with him, but also his relationship with the whole of creation. Christ's relationship with the whole of the universe, his cosmic relationship, is expressed in a hymn in the letter to the Colossians:

He is the image of the unseen God
and the first-born of all creation,
for in him were created
all things in heaven and earth;
everything visible and invisible,
Thrones, Dominations, Sovereignties, Powers –
all things were created through him and for him.
  (Col. 1:15–16)

As Lord, Jesus is not only the head of all creation. All creation was created through him and for him. Everything belongs to him. In a special way we ourselves belong to him. As St Paul said, 'if we live, we live for the Lord; and if we die, we die for the Lord, so that alive or dead we belong to the Lord' (Rom. 14:7). As adults we should gratefully acknowledge our belonging to the Lord and make a formal commitment of our whole lives to him. We can make this commitment in any of our own words. Some people often find this form of words helpful: Lord Jesus Christ, I accept you as my personal Saviour. I am sorry for my sins and ask your forgiveness. I invite you to reign in my heart as Lord. I ask you to fill me and baptise me in your Holy Spirit. I ask you to direct and govern my life and place me where you want me to serve you in your Church under the guidance of your shepherds. (In the next chapter we will consider some of the implications of this commitment.) But, take time now to make your own personal commitment to Jesus your Lord. Ask him to come into your life in a new way.

What does it mean to live under the Lordship of Jesus? Michelle Moran, who is a married woman and a well-known evangelist and leader of Sion Community, tells us how she came to live for the Lord:

AS I GROW OLDER, I AM BECOMING MORE AND MORE AWARE of the fact that conversion is an on-going process in our lives. I made an initial response to Christ at a young people's gathering when I was sixteen years old. At that time I had become increasingly aware of the spiritual void and deep hunger within. Unfortunately I then encountered a religious sect based on an Eastern religion but I found the teaching too intellectual and complex. I was initially attracted to Christianity by other young people. They seemed to be different to me. They had something which was hard to describe but very tangible. Consequently, when they shared with me the basic message of the Gospel, I was totally open and readily prayed a prayer of commitment inviting Jesus to be Lord in my life.

On reflection, I can now see that this was only the beginning. I had publicly declared that Jesus was Lord and that my life was now under 'new management' but I guess I'll spend the rest of my days learning to submit to that Lordship.

Immediately following my youthful conversion experience, I was fortunate enough to be discipled by a very committed group of people. They taught me to pray and read the Scriptures and I gained more insight into the Catholic Church and how it operated. I developed a deep love for the Eucharist and unlike many of my peers, I never found going to Church boring. There just seemed to be so much more to discover and experience. At the same time as growing in knowledge and experience of God and his ways, my leaders also invested time in my personal development. They taught me about what it means to be a disciple, rather than merely a follower and I found the radical aspect of all this very appealing.

Consequently, I became an informed and involved Roman Catholic. I was a teacher in the 6th form of a large local comprehensive school in South London. I also belonged to a couple of groups in our parish; one of which helped to prepare music and liturgy. I had developed a passionate interest in trying to develop our Sunday celebrations. The other parish group which interested me was the newly-formed Justice and Peace group. This time I was attracted by the Kingdom dimension of many of the Justice issues. I've always believed very strongly that Christianity must impact the world and not be merely reserved to what we do in the Church at the weekends. Apart from parochial work I was also, together with my husband, a member of a large central London prayer group which met weekly. We were both involved in a musical capacity and gradually it became evident that I might have something to offer in the area of teaching. Although I felt that I didn't really know all that much, I was able to share with ease my own Christian experience and reflections.

Although I didn't realise it at the time, all this was gradually preparing me and laying the foundation for the next step on my journey of faith. One day, through friends in the parish, we met a priest, Fr Pat Lynch, who shared with us his vision for evangelisation in the Catholic Church. His idea was to have a group of priests, religious and lay people who would travel around the country helping parishes to develop and grow in their mission. I listened attentively and participated in the discussion with enthusiasm, never thinking for a moment that we would be called into such work. However, five months later we were trusting in God and depending upon his providence as we tried to respond to his call in our lives. We sold our house (because we couldn't afford to keep it) and both of us had given up our jobs in order to work 'full time' in the Church.

I don't think that God called us because we were extraordinary in any way. On the contrary, the fact that we seemed to be 'ordinary people' was one of the things which others found attractive. Although both of us had some religious education and formation, neither of us would say that we were theologians or even particularly well versed in the Scriptures or Church teaching. However, God used us powerfully in the proclamation of the Gospel and we were able to witness to the love of Christ as we experienced in through our marriage.

This year marks the tenth anniversary of Sion Community. Obviously there has been much growth in our lives, in the Church and in our Community over the past decade. My husband and I have grown in experience, knowledge, ability and faith. Personally I have been privileged to travel extensively both nationally and internationally preaching and teaching. I have had many opportunities to share my ideas about evangelising from a Catholic perspective and indeed have written a couple of books on the topic. However, I am all too aware that God still has so much more in store for me as I continue to grow in faithfulness and submission to him through the power of the Holy Spirit. In the words of St Paul 'Nothing can happen that will outweigh the supreme advantage of knowing Christ Jesus, my Lord' (Phil. 4:8).

Michelle's testimony reveals how Jesus works in the lives a married couple who come under his Lordship. I will just highlight the main insights:

- Conversion is an ongoing process. We must be open to be converted each day.

- She welcomed the basic message of the Gospel when it was shared with her by other young people.
- Once she accepted Christ as Lord her life 'was under new management'.
- The Lord found her a community of committed people where she was trained in the way of the disciple, reading the Scriptures and praying and growing in knowledge and love of the Church.
- She received a deep love for the Eucharist.
- She developed a passion for 'Kingdom dimension of many of the Justice issues'.
- She discovered a new charism for teaching and sharing her experience as a Christian.
- Providentially she met Fr Pat Lynch and the Sion Community came into being as a new community for evangelisation.
- She recognised that the Lord had been preparing her for this new work in the Church in all that went before.
- She received the grace to live on divine providence, trusting that the God who called her to proclaim his good news would take care of her and all who joined the community.
- She learned in a new way, with St Paul that 'Nothing can happen that will outweigh the supreme advantage of knowing Jesus Christ, my Lord'.

Michelle's testimony makes it very clear that when we accept Jesus as our Lord, when, as she says, 'our life comes under new management', then the Lord is free to do new things, even surprising things in us. And, in the Church today, through Sion Community and through many similar lay led communities the Lord is truly doing great things. That is why we must always praise him for the new communities, the new labourers, which are now at work in the vineyard.

Faith sharing

1. Are you aware of a more personal relationship with Jesus now that you have more consciously accepted him as Lord in your life?
2. Would you be able to see the meaning of your life and the significance of your successes or failures in a new way, in the light of the Lordship of Jesus?
3. How do you see sin in the light of Jesus Christ being Lord?

Scripture reading

The Vatican Council says:

THE DIVINELY REVEALED REALITIES, WHICH ARE CONTAINED and are presented in the text of the sacred Scripture, have been written down under the inspiration of the Holy Spirit. For Holy Mother Church relying on the faith of the apostolic age, accepts as sacred and canonical the books of the Old and the New Testament, whole and entire, with all their parts, on the ground that, written under the inspiration of the Holy Spirit, they have God as their author and have been handed on as such to the Church herself.[12]

We constantly remind ourselves as we read the Scriptures that God is the author of these wonderful books.

Sunday	Acts 9—10
Monday	Acts 11—13
Tuesday	Acts 14—16
Wednesday	Acts 17—19
Thursday	Acts 20—21
Friday	Acts 22—24
Saturday	Acts 25—27

8

Jesus the Lord
sends us the Holy Spirit

God's promise to us is summed up in the words:

I will pour out my spirit on all mankind.
Your sons and your daughters shall prophesy,
your old men shall dream dreams,
and your young men see visions. (Joel 3:1)

The whole of the Bible is the history of how God fulfilled that promise, from his first utterance of the promise until its final fulfilment when God says: 'And now I am making the whole of creation new' (Rev. 21:5). We have looked at some aspects of the promise in chapter 5 – the promise of the New Covenant, the new heart, the promise of living water, and of Christ's abiding presence. In this chapter we want to look more directly at the person of the promise, the person of the Holy Spirit.

In the Creed we say: 'We believe in the Holy Spirit, the Lord the giver of life.' Our first profession is faith in the person of the Spirit. The Holy Spirit is not just a 'good influence', not just the good influence of Jesus. The Holy Spirit is a divine person. He is equal to the Father and equal to the Son. And, as we say in the creed, 'with the Father and the Son he is worshipped and glorified'. Because the Spirit is a person we can have a personal relationship with him. We can know the Spirit. As Jesus promised, 'You know him because he is with you, he is in you' (John 14:18). We can listen to the Holy Spirit, speak with him, follow his guidance, receive his gifts. Most of all we can receive the gift of the very presence of the

Holy Spirit in our hearts and souls. As the Church prays in
the divine office:

Come, Holy Ghost, Creator come
From thy bright heavenly throne,
Come, take possession of our souls,
and make them all thy own.
Thou who are called the Paraclete
Best gift of God above,
The living spring, the living fire,
Sweet unction and true love.

That ancient hymn expresses the heartfelt desire of the Christian heart to be filled with the Spirit of God.

The promise of the Father

Jesus referred to the Spirit as 'the promise of the Father': 'Now
I am sending down to you what my Father has promised' (Luke
24:49). In the sending of the Spirit, God's great promise of our
salvation reaches fulfilment. The promise was expressed in
many different ways in the Bible:

- Behold I am doing a new thing (Isa. 43:19).
- I will give you a new heart and put a new spirit in you
  (Exod. 36:25).
- Deep within them I will plant my law writing it on their
  hearts (Jer. 31:31).
- I will pour out my spirit on all mankind (Joel 3:1).
- If only you knew the gift of God (John 4:10).
- If any man is thirsty, let him come to me!
  Let the man come and drink who believes in me!
  As Scripture says: From his breast shall flow fountains of
  living water. He was speaking of the Spirit which those
  who believed in him were to receive. (John 7:37–39)
- I shall ask the Father, and he will give you another Advo-
  cate to be with you for ever, that Spirit of truth which the
  world can never receive since it neither sees nor knows

him; but you know him because he is with you, he is in you' (John 14:18).

- When he had been at table with them, he told them not to leave Jerusalem, but to wait there for what the Father had promised. 'It is' he said 'what you have heard me speak about: John baptised with water but you, not many days from now, will be baptised with the Holy Spirit' (Acts 1:5).

The Holy Spirit in the life of Jesus

God fulfilled his promise to pour out his Spirit through our Lord Jesus Christ. But before he fulfilled his promise *through* Christ he fulfilled it *in* Christ. Jesus, the 'holy one of God', became the source of the Spirit for us. In the life of Jesus we see a threefold outpouring of the Holy Spirit:

1. THE SPIRIT COMES AT THE CONCEPTION OF JESUS. We express our faith in this coming in words of the Apostles Creed: 'He was conceived by the power of the Holy Spirit and born of the virgin Mary.' The angel had assured Mary: 'The Holy Spirit will come upon you and the power of the Most High will cover you with its shadow' (Luke 1:31). The very humanity of Jesus is the result of the Holy Spirit's creative action in Our Blessed Lady.

2. THE SPIRIT COMES ON JESUS AT HIS BAPTISM AND anoints him as Messiah. The Spirit empowers Jesus for his messianic work of preaching the Gospel and saving us from our sins. It is through the power of the Spirit that Jesus performs all his works. Most of all, it is through the power of the Spirit that Jesus offers himself on the cross to the Father. As Scripture says, 'Christ offered himself as the perfect sacrifice to God through the eternal Spirit' (Heb. 9:14).

3. THE SPIRIT COMES ON THE DEAD JESUS IN THE TOMB AND raises him into the life of the resurrection. St Paul writes:

'This news is about the Son of God who, according to the human nature he took, was a descendant of David: it is about Jesus Christ our Lord who, in the order of the spirit, the spirit of holiness that was in him, was proclaimed Son of God in all his power through his resurrection from the dead' (Rom. 1:4).

In the resurrection Jesus receives the fullness of the Spirit for us. As St Peter said, 'Now raised to the heights by God's right hand, he has received from the Father the Holy Spirit, who was promised, and what you see and hear is the outpouring of that Spirit' (Acts 2:33). God's promise is now fulfilled: the Holy Spirit is poured out. The promise is fulfilled, first of all in the person of Our Lord Jesus Christ. In that fulfilment Christ becomes the New Adam, the source of the renewed and restored humanity. As St Paul said, 'The last Adam became a life-giving Spirit' (1 Cor. 15:45). Tom Smail comments:

THE LAST ADAM, THE ULTIMATE MAN, IS THE ONE WHO HAS been transfigured and sanctified by the Spirit so as to fulfil at last God's purpose for the whole of humanity. As such he is so full of the Spirit of divine self-giving that he pours out upon others his transfigured and fulfilled humanity, so that they also may be changed into sanctified and fulfilled people.[1]

The Church

This is the mystery of Pentecost, the mystery of the Church. The Second Vatican Council made it very clear that the Church is established when the Spirit is poured out:

BY COMMUNICATING HIS SPIRIT to his brothers, called together from all people, Christ made them mystically his own body.[2]

RISING FROM THE DEAD, He sent his life-giving Spirit upon his disciples and through this Spirit has established his body, the Church, as the universal sacrament of salvation.[3]

AFTER BEING LIFTED UP on the cross and glorified, the Lord Jesus poured forth the Spirit whom he had promised and through whom he called and gathered the people of the New Covenant.[4]

The Council teaches that the Church is the direct result of Christ's action of sending the Spirit. Pentecost is the birth of the Church. Just as Jesus himself was born through the power of the Holy Spirit so the Church of Christ is born through that same Holy Spirit. The Church is God's plan for our salvation. We cannot separate Christ from the Church, nor can we separate the Holy Spirit from the Church. Christ established the Church by sending the Spirit. Christ and the Spirit are co-creative of and co-responsible for the Church. It was not God's will to save us simply as individuals. The Vatican Council teaches: 'God has willed to make people holy and save them, not as individuals without any bond or link between them, but rather to make them into a people who might acknowledge him and serve him in holiness.'[5] It is as members of the Church that we are saved and sanctified. The first action of the Spirit is to make us one – one people of God, the one body of Christ, the children of God.

God's Spirit in our hearts

The Spirit is the proof that we have become the children of God. St Paul said: 'The proof that you are sons is that God has sent the Spirit of his Son into our hearts: the Spirit that cries, "Abba, Father", and it is this that makes you a son, you are not a slave any more' (Gal. 4:6). Writing to the Romans, Paul said: 'Every one moved by the Spirit is a son of God. The spirit you received is not the spirit of sons, and it makes us cry out, "Abba, Father". The Spirit himself and our spirit bear united witness that we are children of God' (Rom. 8:15). Paul goes on to say: 'The Spirit of God has made his home in you' (Rom. 8:9). The Spirit is Christ's first gift to us. The Spirit within us enables us to acknowledge what Christ has achieved

for us: 'To all who did accept him he gave power to become
children of God' (John 1:12). We acknowledge that we have
become children of God through Christ when we call God
'Abba'. When we say 'Abba' then 'the Spirit and our spirit bear
united witness that we are children of God'.

We need the Spirit in order to pray 'Abba'. But we also need
the Spirit to acknowledge that Jesus is Lord. St Paul says 'No
one can say "Jesus is Lord" unless he is under the influence of
the Spirit' (1 Cor. 12:3). Our human reason alone, therefore,
cannot give us the assurance that we are children of God. This
assurance can only come through the Spirit. The Spirit brings
to our consciousness the awareness that we are God's children
and prays within us: Abba, Father. In the fine distinction of
Tom Smail we must pray this prayer *for ourselves* but we
cannot pray it *by ourselves*. None of us can decide, simply by
our own reason, to accept God as our loving Father. That
acceptance, that recognition, comes from the presence of the
Holy Spirit in our hearts. In the same way, the Spirit also brings
to our consciousness the fact that Jesus is now seated at the
right hand of the Father and enables us to acknowledge this
mystery by proclaiming 'Jesus Christ is Lord'. The confession
of the Lordship of Jesus comes through the grace of the Spirit's
personal presence in our hearts. Again, we must make this
profession that Jesus is Lord *for ourselves*, but we cannot make
it *by ourselves*. This profession is the work of grace. Without
the grace of faith all the study in the world will not enable a
person to proclaim that Jesus is Lord. As Tom Smail points
out: 'The techniques of biblical scholarship can certainly bring
us to a more accurate appreciation of what the biblical writers
are saying; but, to bring us to the conviction of the truth of
the gospel and a relationship with the God of whom it speaks,
is the prerogative of the Holy Spirit alone.'[6]

Two short phrases, then, highlight the major work of the
Holy Spirit in our hearts. Through the Holy Spirit we can call
God our loving Father, our Abba; through the same Spirit we
can proclaim that Jesus who died for us is now Lord of all.
The Holy Spirit is a praying presence in our hearts, constantly

interceding for us. We should hold on with great confidence to what St Paul tells us about this praying activity of the Spirit in our hearts:

> THE SPIRIT TOO COMES TO HELP US IN OUR WEAKNESS. FOR when we cannot choose words in order to pray properly, the Spirit himself expresses our plea in a way that could not be put into words, and God who knows everything in our hearts knows perfectly well what he means, and that the pleas of the saints expressed by the Spirit are according to the mind of God. (Rom. 8:26–27).

Our hearts are full of prayer, not our own prayer, and not our own very inadequate words of prayer, but the eternal prayer of the Holy Spirit, interceding for us and bringing our deepest needs to our loving Father. The Spirit cries 'Abba'. That is the prayer of Jesus. The Spirit is not the 'son of the Father': Jesus is. The Spirit produces in us the prayer which he produces in the heart of Jesus. Now, in the same Spirit we can pray with Jesus 'Abba, Father'. As André Louf said:

> We received prayer along with grace in our baptism. The state of grace, as we call it, at the level of the heart actually signifies a *state of prayer.* From then on in the profoundest depths of the self, we have a continuing contact with God. God's Holy Spirit has taken us over, has assumed complete possession of us; he has become breath of our breath and Spirit of our spirit. He takes our heart in tow and turns it towards God . . . This state of prayer within us is something we always carry about with us, like a hidden treasure of which we are not consciously aware. Somewhere our heart is going full pelt, but we do not feel it. We are deaf to our praying heart.[7]

Pause for a moment now. Ask the Holy Spirit to come. Listen to his voice as he prays 'Abba, Father'. And, as you join your voice with his in calling God your loving Father proclaim also that Jesus is Lord. Then become aware of the great mystery that the Holy Spirit is praying in your very weakness.

The sanctifying role of the Spirit

The primary role of the Holy Spirit is the sanctification of God's people. As Tom Smail puts it:

> The distinctive work of the Spirit is to communicate to us the life that is in the Father and the Son, so that we actually share and experience it in ourselves. In the Spirit the life that the Father wills and that the Son incarnates is brought over to our side of our relationship with them and begins to reach its destination in us as the first fruits of the whole human race for which it was intended.[8]

When the Spirit of God comes to dwell in us at our baptism he fills us with the whole life of God. We are, in the words of Jesus, reborn of water and the Holy Spirit'. We become the people of the new covenant.

St Thomas Aquinas, 700 years ago, was clearly identifying the new covenant with the Holy Spirit. He wrote: 'The New Covenant consists in the inpouring of the Holy Spirit'[9], and in another commentary he said, 'As the Holy Spirit works in us charity which is the fullness of the Law, he himself is the New Covenant.'[10] God promised to write the law of the new covenant on our hearts: 'This is the covenant I will make with the House of Israel ... Deep within them I will plant my law writing on their hearts' (Jer. 31:34). St Thomas quotes St Augustine who said, 'what else are the divine laws written by God himself on our hearts but the very presence of his Holy Spirit'. In this same article St Thomas says: 'That which is preponderant in the law of the New Covenant and whereon all its efficacy is based, is the grace of the Holy Spirit, which is given through faith in Christ. Consequently the New Law is chiefly the grace itself of the Holy Spirit'.[11] Because the new law is chiefly the grace of the Holy Spirit, St Thomas says that the new law, unlike the old law, justifies us. It makes us holy because the law itself is the very presence of the sanctifying Holy Spirit.

We are the 'people of the new covenant'. That means, we are the people of the Holy Spirit, the people whose interior law of action is the Spirit of God. As Fr Lyonnet wrote: 'The law of the Spirit is by its very nature radically different from the old law. It is no longer a code, even if "given by the Holy Spirit", but a law "accomplished in us by the Holy Spirit"; not a simple, external norm of action, but what no other code of laws as such could be, a principle of action, a new, interior dynamism.'[12] The new law is the sanctifying, dynamic presence of the Holy Spirit. That is why St Paul can say: 'if we live by the Spirit let us walk by the Spirit' (Gal. 5:25). Our Christian morality is not a slavish following of laws; it is a joyful, free response to the Spirit of God who wants to transform us into the perfect image of Christ (Rom. 8:25).

Jesus identified three things which the Spirit would do:

> And when he comes,
> he will show the world how wrong it was,
> about sin,
> about who was in the right,
> and about judgement:
> about sin:
> proved by their refusal to believe in me;
> about who was in the right:
> proved by my going to the Father
> and you seeing me no more;
> about judgement:
> proved by the prince of this world being already
> condemned. (John 16:9–11)

The Holy Spirit convicts us of sin. Scripture says that 'The heart is more devious than any other thing' (Jer. 17:9) The sinful heart cannot admit its sinfulness. It is only the light of the Spirit which can dispel the darkness of sin. The Spirit, who was 'sent among us for the forgiveness of sin', prepares our heart for this gift by enabling us to acknowledge our sinfulness and say with the publican in the temple 'Lord be merciful to me a sinner'. (Luke 18:13). Pope John Paul writes:

IN THIS WAY 'CONVINCING CONCERNING SIN' BECOMES AT the same time a convincing concerning the remission of sins in the power of the Holy Spirit. Peter in his discourse in Jerusalem calls people to conversion, as Jesus called his listeners to conversion at the beginning of his messianic activity. Conversion requires convincing of sin; it includes the interior judgement of the conscience, and this, being a proof of the action of the Spirit of truth in man's inmost being, becomes at the same time a new beginning of the bestowal of grace and love: 'Receive the Holy Spirit.' Thus in the 'convincing concerning sin' we discover a double gift: the gift of the truth of conscience and the gift of the certainty of redemption. The Spirit of truth is the Counsellor.[13]

The Holy Spirit, then, is the new covenant; he is the guarantee that we are the children of God; by enabling us to call God 'Abba' and proclaim that 'Jesus is Lord' he simultaneously fills us with the life of God and convicts us of our sinfulness so that we can turn to God and have our sins forgiven. The Holy Spirit is our divine friend and protector; he is our divine guide and our sanctifier; he is our divine encourager and comforter. And he wants to have a loving, personal relationship with each of us. My brother Sean, a Redemptorist priest in Washington, came into a new personal relationship with the Holy Spirit one night as he was praying about the troubles in Northern Ireland. For the past 20 years he has been working through the American Congress for political action which would address the deep causes of conflict in Northern Ireland. His prayer was for peace. The Lord answered his prayer in a very personal way. He kept him awake one night filling his heart with praise and gratitude and giving him this prayer of commitment in his heart:

All powerful-Gentle
Faithful-Gracious
Crucified-Risen
L I V I N G
Lord Jesus:
Send me your Spirit.

Lord of History,
Lord of the world
Lord of Ireland
Lord of my heart
Pour out your Spirit upon me.

Lord Jesus:
I am an empty vessel,
parched and thirsty,
waiting to be filled.
Fill me with your living water
that I may never thirst again.

Risen Jesus
Baptise me in your Spirit
so that I can truly call God,
'Abba', Father.
Come Holy Spirit, come
'Take possession of my soul
and make it all thy own'.

Come living flame divine
Consume this heart of mine
Come holy breath of God
Breathe on me your life.

Come dwell with me
Holy Paraclete,
My Counsellor and my Guide
Come, heal my heart and mind.

This prayer, 'bubbled up', as he said, within him and kept him in the presence of God the whole night. It gave him a whole new relationship with God. A personal relationship. Jesus wants each of us to have an intimate, personal relationship with the Father, a loving acknowledgement that he is Lord and a grateful awareness that the Holy Spirit in our hearts is 'the Lord, the giver of life'.

Faith sharing

1. Do you see yourself as an individual, who believes, relating to other believing individuals, or do you have a sense of yourself as being a member of the body of Christ, a member of the Church of Christ?
2. How would you describe your vision of the Church?
3. Do you have a personal relationship with the Holy Spirit?

Scripture reading

The Vatican Council says:

THE CHURCH FORCEFULLY AND SPECIFICALLY EXHORTS ALL the Christian faithful, especially those who live the religious life, to learn 'the surpassing knowledge of Jesus Christ' (Phil. 3:8) by frequent reading of the divine Scriptures. Ignorance of the Scriptures is ignorance of Christ. Therefore let them go gladly to the sacred text itself, whether in the sacred liturgy, which is full of the divine words, or in devout reading, or in such suitable exercises and various other helps which, with the approval and guidance of the pastors of the Church, are happily spreading everywhere today.[14]

Sunday	Romans 1—3
Monday	Romans 4—7
Tuesday	Romans 8—11
Wednesday	Romans 12—16
Thursday	1 Corinthians 1—4
Friday	1 Corinthians 5—9
Saturday	1 Corinthians 10—13

9

The gifts of the Holy Spirit

In the last chapter we reflected on the sanctifying role of the Holy Spirit. He is the Lord the giver of life, our eternal life. He comes to us so that we can be reborn as children of God. In our hearts he cries out 'Abba, Father'; he enables us to proclaim that Jesus is Lord. He is, as St Thomas Aquinas said, 'the new covenant'. In the words of the liturgy: 'he is sent among us for the forgiveness of our sins.' At one and the same time he convicts us of sin and, as we said in the Mass, 'he himself is the forgiveness of sins'. All this work of the Holy Spirit is for our sanctification.

We are called to be holy. But holiness for us comes through our sharing fully in Christ's mission, doing Christ's work on earth in the way in which he himself did it, namely through the power of the Holy Spirit. The Vatican Council, for instance, said that, 'Priests will acquire holiness in their own distinctive way by exercising their functions sincerely and tirelessly in the Spirit of Christ'.[1] The other members of the Church acquire holiness by the way in which they live out their vocation, married, single or religious, in union with the Spirit of Jesus. The Spirit who was given to us for our sanctification, (*sanctifying grace*) is also given to us so that we can make Christ known to others (*charismatic grace*). In the fourth eucharistic prayer the Church prays:

That we might live no longer for ourselves but for him,
he sent the Holy Spirit from you, Father,
as his first gift to those who believe,
to complete his work on earth
and bring us the fullness of grace.

The Spirit comes 'to complete Christ's work'. This he does in and through each member of Christ's body, the Church. And just as the Spirit empowered Jesus for his work, when he anointed him at the Jordan, so the Spirit empowers us when he anoints us, especially in the sacrament of confirmation. Jesus promised that empowerment. He said: 'John baptised with water but you, not many days from now, will be baptised with the Holy Spirit . . . you will receive power when the Holy Spirit comes and then you will be my witnesses' (Acts 1:5, 8). A young man in Jos, in Northern Nigeria, gave me a vivid illustration of this. He was selling crocodile skin bags and purses. I went up to his stall with a priest friend and we began to bargain. To our surprise he would not lower his price and we were about to move on to another stall. 'One moment', he said, 'I am not here to sell bags.' At that he reached beneath his stall and took out two leaflets. He gave me a leaflet and he handed a leaflet to my friend. As he did so he said to my friend, who was a professional theologian, 'Have you received the new heart?' Somewhat taken aback my friend replied, 'I think I have'. The young man responded immediately: 'what do you mean: you think you have? If you have you know, if you don't know, you haven't!' My friend, now quite flustered, said 'well, have you received the new heart?' The young man said, with great confidence, 'Yes, I have'. To which my friend responded, 'how do you know?' And with calm assurance the young man replied 'because I have the power to witness to Jesus'. Jesus had promised: 'you will receive power when the Spirit comes and then you will be my witnesses.' The Spirit had come. The proof was in the fact that he was an evangelist. He was trying to make Christ known.

This empowerment of the Holy Spirit manifests itself in what St Paul called charisms. Paul coined this Greek word, which means 'work of grace', to describe the activity of the Holy Spirit in the lives of Christians. He wrote to the Corinthians:

THERE IS A VARIETY OF GIFTS (CHARISMS), BUT ALWAYS THE same Spirit; there are all sorts of service to be done, but always to the same Lord; working in all sorts of different ways in different people, it is the same God who is working in all of them. The particular way in which the Spirit is given to each person is for a good purpose. One may have the gift of preaching with wisdom, given him by the Spirit; another the gift of preaching instruction given by the same Spirit; and another the gift of faith given by the same Spirit; another again the gift of healing, through this one Spirit; one, the power of miracles; another, prophecy; another the gift of recognising spirits; another the gift of tongues and another the ability to interpret them. All these are the work of one and the same Spirit, who distributes different gifts to different people just as he chooses. (1 Cor. 12:4–11)

We call these gifts of the Spirit 'charismatic gifts or graces'.

The Holy Spirit gives us two distinct graces:

1. SANCTIFYING GRACE This grace makes us the children of God. This is the gift of eternal life. Our eternal salvation depends on this grace.

2. CHARISMATIC GRACE This grace enables us to serve others. It empowers us to fulfill the mission that Christ has entrusted to each of us. Like the young man in Jos it enables us to say: 'I have the power to witness to Jesus.'

We need both graces. Through sanctifying grace we *live in union with God*; through charismatic grace we *work in union with God*. To put it another way: through sanctifying grace the Spirit works in us to keep us united to God; through charismatic grace the Spirit works in us to keep us serving the Kingdom of God.

In his Apostolic Letter announcing the Jubilee of the year 2000, as we begin the third millennium of the birth of Christ, Pope John Paul II points to the signs of hope in the world today. The charisms of the Spirit are one. 'In the Church', he writes, 'the signs of hope include a greater attention to the voice of the Spirit through the acceptance of charisms and the promotion of the laity, a deeper commitment to the cause of Christian unity and the increased interest in dialogue with other religions and with contemporary culture.'[2] It is surely significant that the pope sees in the reception given to the charisms of the faithful one of the great signs of hope as the Church approaches the third millennium. For centuries there was a strong conviction in the Church that the charisms should not be expected in our day. Even in the Vatican Council this opinion was voiced by Cardinal Rufini. Killian McDonald writes:

> IN CARDINAL RUFINI'S VIEW, BOTH HISTORY AND EXPERIENCE contradict the notion that in our day many of the faithful are gifted with charisms, and that such people can be relied on to make a significant contribution to the upbuilding of the Church. On the contrary, he insisted, such gifts today are 'extremely rare and altogether exceptional'. In his view it is obvious that charisms have no important role to play in the life of the modern Church.[3]

That view of Rufini did not prevail. In fact, the Council rejected it in most emphatic terms. In its major document on the Church it teaches:

> IT IS NOT ONLY THROUGH THE SACRAMENTS AND CHURCH ministries that the same Holy Spirit sanctifies and leads the People of God and enriches it with virtues. Allotting his gifts "to everyone according to his will" (1 Cor. 12:11), he distributes special graces among the faithful of every rank. By these gifts he makes them fit and ready to undertake various tasks and offices advantageous for the renewal and upbuilding of the Church, according to the words of the Apostle: "The manifestation of the Spirit is given to everyone for profit" (1 Cor. 12:7). These charismatic gifts, whether they be the most outstanding or the more simple and widely diffused, are to be received with thanksgiving and consolation, for they are exceedingly suitable and useful for the needs of the Church.[4]

The prophetic nature of this statement is highlighted by the fact that today, as we approach the year 2000, John Paul sees in the reception given to the charisms one of the great signs of hope in the Church.

What is a charism? Francis Sullivan sj proposes this definition: 'A charism can be described as a grace-given capacity and willingness for some kind of service that contributes to the renewal of and upbuilding of the Church'.[5] Unlike 30 years ago, when Cardinal Rufini was asking for the elimination of all mention of charisms from the texts of the Vatican Council documents, the Church today has a broad experience of the charisms at work in men and women in every walk of life. Indeed, in his very first encyclical Pope John Paul II wrote:

> THE POWERS OF THE SPIRIT, THE GIFTS OF THE SPIRIT, AND the fruits of the Holy Spirit are revealed in men. The present-day Church seems to repeat with ever greater fervour and with holy insistence: Come, Holy Spirit! Come! Come! Heal our wounds, our strength renew; On our dryness pour your dew; Wash the stains of guilt away; Mend the stubborn heart and will; Melt the frozen, warm the chill; Guide the hearts that go astray.[6]

This 'holy insistence' in calling on the Spirit to come has become a transforming prayer in the lives millions of men and women throughout the Church. They have found their lives changed; they witness to a deeper experience of God; they begin to use new gifts of the Spirit and become involved in ministries at every level in their communities. Their transforming experience is frequently called 'baptism in the Spirit'.

Baptism in the Spirit

Jesus promised: 'I tell you solemnly once again, if two of you on earth agree to ask anything at all, it will be granted to you by my Father in heaven. For where two or three meet in my name, I shall be there with them' (Matt. 18:19–20). Many people have begun to act on this promise in new ways. They meet in small prayer groups. They acknowledge the presence of Jesus. They confess that Jesus alone baptises in the Holy Spirit. They accept Jesus as their Lord and Saviour and commit their lives to him. Then they pray over each other, asking the Father, in Jesus name, to fill them afresh with the Spirit, to 'baptise them in the Holy Spirit'. And he does. The Father honours the promise of Jesus and pours out the Spirit afresh. They pray not only for a fresh outpouring of the Spirit but for the release of all the gifts of the Spirit which were already given in baptism and in confirmation.

People often explain their experience in this way. They were baptised as infants and confirmed at a young age. While recognising that the sacraments brought them the new life of Christ and the gift of the Spirit they also admit that they had not personally, as free and mature adults, ratified that Christian commitment which was made on their behalf by their sponsors. They may have lived for many years, as practising Catholics, without ever saying: 'Jesus I accept you as my Lord and Saviour and I ask you to unite me more deeply to yourself by filling me with your Spirit. Jesus, release within me all the many gifts of the Spirit you gave me when I was baptised and confirmed.' When a person is led to say this prayer and make this commitment in the presence of others, and asks others to pray over him or her for the outpouring of the Spirit, the Lord always answers this prayer. Sometimes the answer can be quite dramatic. Some people witness to great experiences of peace and joy and inner healing; they speak of knowing God's forgiving love in a new way and of beginning to live their Christian lives in a new way. Others say that they had no sensible experience at all and yet they knew, deep down, that something very profound had happened. They had opened themselves to the Lord in a new way and he had come to them. The fruit of his visit only appears gradually.

Fr Bob Poole witnesses to the gradual development of 'baptism in the Spirit' in his own life:

ALTHOUGH I WAS BAPTISED IN THE SPIRIT IN 1978, I DIDN'T come into the exercise of the gifts until 8 years later. I had an intellectual and psychological block against the gift of tongues. I used to argue to myself that Paul did not seem to place too much value on that particular charism, so it wasn't really necessary to my spiritual growth; I could get by very easily without it. The trouble was that none of the other charisms seemed to be working very obviously in my life either. I certainly never received prophecies, nothing of a particularly healing nature happened to people when I prayed with them. I think now, looking back, that even though I had entered more fully into life in the Spirit, the Spirit was still operating at a very low level of power in my life, because basically I still wanted to be in control. Tongues was for me a sign of being 'out of control', as well as making me look rather foolish, so I was pretending to myself that I did not need it; naturally, then, nothing happened when I (occasionally and somewhat half-heartedly) prayed to receive the gift of tongues.

Then in 1988 I went to the seminary to train for the priesthood. There I met two students who had a very powerful experience of the power of the Spirit delivering them from very serious bondage in their lives. They introduced me to a level of life in the Spirit that I had never experienced before. Up to then my experiences had been very cosy, mediocre, and under my control. These two seminarians also introduced me to different dimensions of the power of praise. Up to then my experience of praise and worship had been like my experience of the power of the Spirit, very mediocre. I came to realise that praise was something the Spirit did in me as I surrendered myself to him, and I began to 'let myself go' more in my praise and worship, focusing not on myself but on the Lordship of Christ. As I was praying in this way one evening over one of the other seminarians, I suddenly 'took off' into praying in tongues. I was suddenly taken over by a sense of God's awesomeness, his glory and his majesty, and my spirit exulted to the point where words were simply not enough to express what I was feeling, and 'overflowed' as it were into a gift of tongues. I suddenly understood why Mary had proclaimed: 'My soul magnifies the Lord and my spirit exults in God my Saviour' (Luke 1:47). I also knew then what Paul was on about when he wrote 'when we do not know how to pray as we should, the Spirit intercedes for us with sighs too deep for words' (Rom. 8:26).

In actual fact, so caught up was I in the experience that it was only when I sat down again afterwards that I became conscious of what had happened. I remember saying to myself with amazement: 'my goodness, I've actually prayed in tongues, for the first time in my life.' It was almost as if God had to 'catch me off guard' as it were and visit me with the gift, when my psychological defences were down, and I was 'looking elsewhere', i.e. at the Lord and not at myself.

Once I made the breakthrough into 'tongues', I found that other charisms followed readily. I was soon prophesying, and there were noticeable effects of God's healing power when I prayed with people. I found there was a perceptible anointing on my preaching as well. I understood now, as I would have ridiculed hitherto, why tongues has sometimes been called the 'gateway' to the other gifts. If one is not willing to surrender to the 'least of the gifts' for fear of losing control and looking foolish, one is not likely to surrender to the other gifts either.

Fr Bob's testimony highlights several spiritual principles:

- The Spirit's action my take a long time before a person experiences a breakthrough into the gifts.
- Wanting to retain control, in every situation, and not surrendering to the Lord are big obstacles to the development of life in the Spirit.
- The desire to remain firmly in control results from focusing on self instead of on the Lord.
- When we focus totally on the Lord the Spirit is free to do a new work within us.

- We should not treat the gifts of the Spirit as a spiritual supermarket, picking and choosing among the gifts. We should follow the advice of St Paul 'hope for the spiritual gifts' (1 Cor. 14:1).
- We should welcome the gift of tongues. Again, St Paul said 'While I should like you all to have the gift of tongues ...' (1 Cor. 14:5).
- Bob discovered that once he yielded to the gift of tongues other gifts began to manifest themselves in his ministry.
- The new gifts were gifts for others, for his work as a priest to bring the experience of God's healing love to people.

Two basic attitudes are necessary for coming into a fuller life in the Spirit:

1. We must be convinced that God loves us and that 'he has poured his love into our hearts by the Holy Spirit which has been given to us' (Rom. 5:5).
2. We must have a great expectation that when we ask the Father in Jesus' name for the renewal of the gift of the Spirit within us, for a fresh outpouring of the Spirit in our lives, the Father answers that prayer, especially when we ask through the prayers of others: 'how much more will the heavenly Father give the Holy Spirit to those who ask him' (Luke 11:13).

Praying over each other

The Holy Spirit has taught us in these past few decades that when a group of people gather in the name of the Lord and pray over each other for a fresh outpouring of the Holy Spirit they receive great blessings. This is not the place to discuss why this prayer should be so blessed. Suffice it to say that if you make a new commitment to Jesus as your Lord and Saviour, and if you ask a group of Christians to pray with you for a new blessing of the Spirit you will get it. When you gather in a group to pray, symbolise your unity of purpose by gathering around the person. In a prayerful spirit gently impose hands on him or her, and ask the Lord to pour out the Holy Spirit. Ask Jesus to give to each person:

- a new sense of the presence of God as Father
- a new faith in and new awareness of Jesus as Lord
- a new sense of being empowered by the Holy Spirit for witnessing to Jesus
- a new devotion to the Holy Scripture and, for Catholics, a new devotion to the Blessed Sacrament and our Blessed Lady
- a new prayer of praise and gratitude to God in the heart
- a fresh outpouring of the gifts of the Spirit, especially those gifts which are appropriate to one's responsibilities, namely parenthood, teaching or nursing, liturgical responsibilities such as reader, eucharistic minister, music ministry etc.
- freedom from all inhibitions which prevent one from witnessing to Christ
- healing of all inner wounds and hurts
- healing of any physical or psychological sickness
- a blessing to share with one's family and friends

Faith sharing

1. Do you have a desire for a new infilling with the Holy Spirit?
2. Can you share one instance where you sought to use a gift of the Spirit and brought the Good News to someone?
3. Can you recall how fear or self-doubt inhibited you from sharing your faith.

Scripture reading

The Vatican Council says: 'Sacred Scripture is the speech of God as it is put down in writing under the breath of the Holy

Spirit.'[7] Our reverence for Scripture is due to our faith that these are God's words to us.

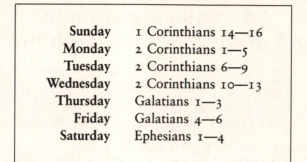

Sunday	1 Corinthians 14—16
Monday	2 Corinthians 1—5
Tuesday	2 Corinthians 6—9
Wednesday	2 Corinthians 10—13
Thursday	Galatians 1—3
Friday	Galatians 4—6
Saturday	Ephesians 1—4

10

'We will come to him
and make our home with him'

When I reflect on all the great promises which God has made
to us through Christ I always feel that this is the greatest:

> If anyone loves me he will keep my word,
> and my Father will love him,
> and we shall come to him
> and make our home with him. (John 14:23)

When I hear that promise I have the same question that Mary
had when she heard that she had been chosen to be the mother
of God: how can this be? How can the all-holy Father and his
Son, Jesus Christ, come and make their home with me? If I ask
that question, I will get the same answer that Mary got: 'The
Holy Spirit will come upon you.' It is in the coming of the Holy
Spirit that the Father and the Son take up their residence in
our hearts. As St Paul said: 'the love of God has been poured
into our hearts by the Holy Spirit which has been given to us'
(Rom. 5:5).

The indwelling presence

The Vatican Council said: 'In reality it is only in the mystery
of the Word made flesh that the mystery of man truly becomes
clear.'[1] The 'mystery of man', the mystery of each man and
woman, is this profound presence of God in the human heart.
We know about this presence because Christ has revealed it to
us. Without revelation we would never have known this amazing truth which should transform our image of God and our

way of relating to God. Too often we may have an image of 'an absent God' or even of 'an uninterested God'. God is in his distant heaven and we must try to get his attention each day by our prayers. Yet, Christ has revealed to us that 'God is closer to us than we are to ourselves'. St Augustine wrote:

> TOO LATE HAVE I LOVED YOU, O BEAUTY SO ANCIENT AND so new, too late have I loved you! Behold, you were within me, while I was outside; it was there I sought you, and, a deformed creature, rushed headlong upon these things of beauty which you have made. You were with me, but I was not with you. They kept me far from you, those fair things which, if they were not in you, would not exist at all. You have called to me, and have cried out, and have shattered my deafness. You blazed forth with light, and have shone upon me, and you have put blindness to flight! You have sent forth fragrance, and I have drawn my breath, and I pant after you. I have tasted you, and I hunger and thirst after you. You have touched me, and I have burned for your peace.[2]

Augustine's liberating discovery was that the God whom he sought was not at a distance. God was within him. Augustine became aware not only that God was within, but also that he himself was without: 'you were within me, while I was outside.' If we do not dwell happily with God who is within us, we begin to live outside ourselves – escaping from the God within, but also escaping from ourselves.

'God is love', St John tells us. God is love itself. This means that at the very centre of our being, an inexhaustible source of divine love resides. Regrettably we often keep a safe distance from that love. Indeed, our relationship with the God of love is often one of fear. How often does God have to tell us in the Bible not to be afraid! God reveals himself to us as love itself, and we often relate to him as if he were hostile. George Herbert caught this fear well in his poem:

Love bade me welcome; yet my soul drew back,
    Guilty of dust and sin.
But quick-eyed Love, observing me grow slack
    From my first entrance in,
Drew nearer to me, sweetly questioning,
    If I lacked anything.

In the presence of totally giving and forgiving Love the human spirit 'draws back'. We are unworthy; we are uncertain. Have we really got a right to enter that inner sanctuary of our heart where God dwells? That is the problem. It is one thing to believe that God dwells in heaven; it is quite another thing to believe that that same holy God dwells in one's heart. It is much easier to relate to God 'up in his heaven' than to relate to God 'deep in our heart'. This problem can only be resolved by living faith. We believe that, 'Through Christ we have access in one Spirit to the Father' (Eph. 2:18). As we pray in the Mass, 'We thank you for counting us worthy to stand in your presence and serve you.' By ourselves we have no right to come into God's presence; through Christ and in his Spirit we are invited and received into his presence. The presence of the Holy Trinity in our hearts is the beginning here on earth of our eternal union with God in heaven. That divine presence within us gives us a new perspective, a Christian perspective on everything outside us. If the creator of all dwells in our hearts the significance of every created thing is relativised. Nothing created, no person, no thing, can become the final goal of a person's life. As St Augustine said: 'you have made us for yourself, O Lord, and our hearts will find no rest until they rest in you.' The God who made us and for whom we exist has made his home in our hearts. That is the source of our human dignity. Even when we sin we do not lose that dignity. God is ever ready to receive us back into a loving union with himself. He never withdraws his gifts and he never ceases to love us. A confrère of mine bears eloquent witness to God's abiding fidelity. He writes:

'I WAS A LAICISED PRIEST, DISPENSED FROM MY RELIGIOUS

vows. Although I had a good job I had never really come to terms with my new status as a lay Catholic. Years ago I had known the Lord at a fairly deep level but now it was almost as if he didn't exist. I barely went to Mass on Sunday, but that was all. No prayer. No sacraments for over five years. My faith seemed dead.

My mother died, and as the eldest son, I had to make all the funeral arrangements. The Requiem Mass was to take place at our local parish church. Family and friends would be there. I hadn't been to that church since I left the priesthood as I was too well known there. I went to Mass elsewhere so no one knew that I abstained from Holy Communion. I could hardly stay away from the funeral Mass, but what about Communion? Should I harden my heart, play the coward and make a bad Communion. I could never do that. Should I simply abstain? But this was my mother's funeral! How could I not enter into it fully? There was, of course, a third option: a good Confession. That sent a shiver up my spine. Could I really go after all I'd done, after all these years? The prospect was not a little daunting. Could I even make a sincere Confession? I felt profoundly disturbed. What I didn't realise was that the 'Hound of Heaven' was at work. He wanted me to enter into myself. My faith was certainly not dead. But I felt so weak, so frightened.

Two days later I was walking down the road near my home when I had the most extraordinary experience. Suddenly, without any warning, I felt the Lord was very near. His presence was almost tangible. He was, as it were, bursting to enter my heart, making me an offer I couldn't refuse. The Lord I had once known and loved, the Lord who still loved me and had never stopped loving me! Did Saul feel like this on the road to Damascus? A kind of happiness flooded into my soul. Yes, I would make that Confession come what may.

The evening before the funeral I went to Westminster cathedral clutching my long list of mortal sins feeling dreadfully nervous and hoping the light in the Confessional would be on so that I could read. It wasn't! I blurted out my Confession as best I could, experiencing now what so many penitents feel and heard the beautiful words 'I absolve you from your sins'. 'For your penance' the priest said, 'receive Holy Communion at the Mass just beginning.' 'Is that all, Father?' 'Yes. Go in peace.' What was I trying to do? Pay for my sins? Didn't I know that they had already been paid for?

What did I feel as I left the Confessional? Like someone emerging from a deep, dark dungeon into the warmth and brightness of a summer's day. I felt as if chains that had held me captive for so long were broken at last. I was FREE. Let no one ever convince you that Jesus didn't come to free the captive. That is not just figurative language. I know it is literally true because I was experiencing it. I had met the Lord. He had returned to re-establish a relationship that was deeper and more intense than ever before.

The Lord never does things by halves. In due course he gave me the incredible invitation to return to my religious Congregation and the priesthood. He waited for my 'Yes' or 'No'. There was to be no compulsion. Only I could give the answer and it had to be given freely. Naturally I hesitated. Would the Congregation have me back? The Lord re-assured me. Never did he let me feel like a second class citizen. I was someone who was loved and wanted and valued. When I gave my 'Yes' doors began to open, doors I had thought were shut for ever. But that is another story.

It is now ten years since my friend rejoined our Congregation and came back to the priesthood. The provincial at the time discerned that God was calling him back into the priesthood and he welcomed him back. His testimony highlights what we know to be so true of the Lord's way with his wayward followers:

- The moment of grace came through the death of his mother.
- He felt that 'the Lord was very near'.

- His presence was 'almost tangible'.
- He felt that the Lord was 'bursting' to enter his heart.
- Those years in the wilderness, where he tried to live without the Lord, were suddenly over.
- Christ had returned to set him free.
- It all began with the inspiration to make a good Confession.
- He discovered that the 'Hound of Heaven' was at work and that 'he wanted me to enter into myself'.
- As he entered into himself he discovered that the God whom he once knew and loved was waiting for him.
- God had never left him.
- He knew, through a liberating personal experience of conversion, the truth that Christ had died for all his sins and that all he had to do was to return, to enter into himself and find God waiting to welcome him and restore him to his friendship.
- He experienced 'a relationship that was deeper and more intense than ever before'.

The two hands of God

God the Father, according to the saying of St Ireneaus in the third century, has two hands: the hand of the eternal Word, Christ our Lord and the hand of the Holy Spirit. With these two hands God the Father does all his work. The Father works very effectively within us because Christ and the Spirit are at work in our hearts. This work of the Holy Trinity is beautifully summed up in the letter to the Ephesians:

THIS, THEN IS WHAT I PRAY, KNEELING BEFORE THE FATHER, from whom every family, whether spiritual or natural, takes its name. Out of his infinite glory, may he (God the Father) give you power through his Spirit for your hidden self to grow strong, so that Christ may live in your hearts through faith, and then, planted in love and built on love, you will with all the saints have strength to grasp the breadth and the length, the height and the depth; until, knowing the love of Christ, which is beyond all knowledge, you are filled with the utter fullness of God. (Eph. 3:14–19).

Through the gift of God our Father, the Holy Spirit strengthens us, renews our inner being, and Christ comes to dwell in our heart through faith. St Paul says: 'Didn't you realise that you were God's temple and the Holy Spirit was living among you?' (1 Cor. 3:16).

In presenting this mystery of the indwelling presence of God in our hearts Scripture also presents the mystery in another way. God not only lives in us, but we also live in God. St Paul can say: 'the life you have is hidden with Christ in God' (Eph. 3:3). In his famous speech in Athens, Paul said that God is not far from anyone because 'it is in him that we live, and move, and exist' (Acts 17:28). And St John says, 'Whoever keeps his commandments lives in God and God lives in him. We know that he lives in us by the Spirit that he has given us' (1 John 3:24). We live and move and have our being in God. But God shows his infinite love for us by living in us, by making us his temple, the home of his Son Jesus Christ.

In the light of this revelation that God dwells in us and that we dwell in him we can ask this question: where does self really exist? We have the biblical answer to this question: self exists in God. We do not exist in a vacuum; nor do we simply exist in the visible, created world. Our very being is immersed in God who is the source and the ground of all being. In the biblical perspective we have this extraordinary reciprocal indwelling – God dwelling in us and we dwelling in God. St Paul struggled to express this revelation: 'I live now not with my own life but with the life of Christ who lives in me' (Gal. 2:20).

Pause now for a while and reflect on how you see yourself. Do you see yourself as immersed in God, 'living, moving and existing in God'.

Faith sharing

1. What difference does the awareness that God the Father and Jesus Christ, his Son, dwell in your heart make to the way you interpret your daily life?
2. What happens to this awareness of God within you when you know that you have sinned in some way?
3. What has helped you during the week to become more aware of the indwelling presence of the Holy Trinity?

Scripture reading

The Vatican Council says: 'The Word of God, which is the power of God for salvation to everyone who has faith (cf Rom. 1:16), is set forth and displays its power in a most wonderful way in the writings of the New Testament.'[3] Each day as you read the New Testament you are in personal contact with this power of God.

Sunday	Ephesians 5—6
Monday	Philippians
Tuesday	Colossians
Wednesday	1 Thessalonians
Thursday	2 Thessalonians
Friday	1 Timothy
Saturday	2 Timothy

11

Life in abundance

Jesus described the purpose of his mission in this way: 'I have come so that they may have life and have it to the full' (John 10:10). This fullness of life which Christ brings us is the gift of God our Father. As the Church prays in the third eucharistic prayer: 'Father, you alone are holy and all creation rightly gives you praise. All life, all holiness comes from you through your Son Jesus Christ our Lord, by the working of the Holy Spirit.' God our Father is the creator of all life. Everything that is, from the greatest to the least, owes its being to the creative love of the Father. The Father of all life rejoices in the life he creates. Death was never part of his creative designs. As the Scriptures assure us:

> Death was not God's doing,
> he takes no pleasure in the extinction of the living.
> To be – for this he created all . . .
> God did make man imperishable,
> he made him in the image of his own nature;
> it was the devil's envy that brought death into the world,
> as those who are his partners will discover.
>   (Wis. 1:13–14; 2:23–24)

Pope John Paul II, in his encyclical on the Value and Inviolability of Human Life (*Evangelium Vitae*) writes:

THE GOSPEL OF LIFE, PROCLAIMED IN THE BEGINNING WHEN man was created in the image of God for a destiny of full and perfect life (cf Gen. 2:7; Wis. 9:2–3), is contradicted by the painful experience of death which enters the world and casts its long shadow of meaninglessness over man's existence. Death came into the world as a result of the devil's envy (cf Gen. 3:1, 4–5) and the sin of our first parents (cf Gen. 2:17, 3:17–19). And death entered it in a violent way, through the killing of Abel by his brother Cain: 'And when they were in the field, Cain rose up against his brother Abel, and killed him.' (Gen. 4:8)[1]

In the Scripture God is clearly seen as the creator of life while man, in the person of Cain, is clearly presented as the perpetrator of death. The destructive, anti-life consequences of the sin of Adam and Eve are now visible in the envy and hatred in the heart of Cain which led him to murder his brother. Long before Abel suffered physical death at the hands of his brother, Cain had already suffered spiritual death. The *Catechism of the Catholic Church* comments: 'In the account of Abel's murder by his brother Cain, the Scripture reveals the presence of anger and envy in man, consequences of original sin, from the beginning of human history. Man has become the enemy of his fellow man.'[2]

This hostility to life, evidenced by envy, anger, enmity and ultimately murder, is the devil's work. The devil seeks to destroy what God has done. That is why St John says: 'It was to undo all that the devil has done that the Son of God appeared' (John 3:8). The life which the devil set out to destroy was already created in and through and for Christ: 'Through him all things came to be, not one thing had its being but through him. All that came to be had life in him' (John 1:4). The evil arrogance of the devil is clearly seen not just in the individual murder of Abel, but in his attempt to destroy the very gift of life itself, the gift which comes to us through Christ by the working of the Holy Spirit.

Jesus: true life

The Gospel of life is the Gospel of Jesus Christ because Jesus, as he says of himself is 'the life': 'I am the Way, the Truth and the Life' (John 14:6). Jesus' friend Martha said to him: 'If you had been here my brother would not have died, but I know that, even now, whatever you ask of God, he will grant you.' In response to the distraught Martha Jesus proclaimed: 'I am the resurrection. If anyone believes in me, even though he dies he will live, and whoever lives and believes in me will never die' (John 11:25). As John says, Jesus is 'the Word, who is life' (1 John 1:1). 'That life was made visible to us: we saw it and we are giving testimony, telling you of the eternal life which was with the Father and has been made visible to us' (1 John 1:2). Pope John Paul writes: 'By the gift of the Spirit, this same life has been bestowed on us. It is in being destined to life in its fullness, to "eternal life", that every person's earthly life acquires its full meaning.'[3] Jesus has come that we may have that eternal life, that life in abundance. We were chosen for this life before the world came into being. As Scripture says:

Before the world was made, God chose us, chose in Christ,
to be holy and spotless, and to live through love in his
presence,
determining that we should become his adopted children,
through Jesus Christ,
for his own kind purposes,
to make us praise the glory of his grace,
his free gift to us in the Beloved,
in whom through his blood, we gain our freedom, the
forgiveness of our sins. (Eph. 1:4–7)

This eternal choice of God whereby each of us is known and chosen and loved by God 'before the world was made' constitutes the very ground of our dignity as human beings. St Gregory of Nyssa, one of the greatest theologians of the early Church, wrote: 'Man, as a being, is of no account; he is dust, grass, vanity. But once he is adopted by the God of the universe as a son, he becomes part of the family of that Being, whose excellence and greatness no one can see, hear or understand. What words, thoughts or flight of the spirit can praise the superabundance of this grace? Man surpasses his nature: mortal, he becomes eternal; human, he becomes divine.'[4] And because God adopts each person as his beloved son or daughter, God wants each one to live with his eternal life – to have life in abundance. Pope John Paul says: 'The life which God bestows upon man is much more than mere existence in time. It is a drive towards fullness of life; it is the seed of existence which transcends the very limits of time: "For God created man for incorruption, and made him in the image of his own eternity" ' (Wis. 2:23).[5]

We have been created for life, for an everlasting life. Our response to God for his gift of life to us should always be one of praise and gratitude. The Holy Spirit teaches us in the psalms to cultivate this gratitude to God for the gift of life and to thank him for the wonder of our own, unique self:

It was you who created my inmost self,
and put me together in my mother's womb;
for all these mysteries I thank you:
for the wonder of myself, the wonder of your works.
(Ps. 139:14)

We thank God for 'the wonder of ourselves'. In order to cultivate this gratitude for ourselves we need to foster in ourselves what Pope John Paul II calls 'a contemplative outlook'. This, he writes, is 'the outlook of those who see life in its deeper meaning, who grasp its utter gratuitousness, its beauty and its invitation to freedom and responsibility. It is the outlook of those who do not presume to take possession of reality but instead accept it as a gift, discovering in all things the reflection of the Creator and seeing in every person his living image.'[6] The gift of fullness of life evokes the response of fullness of gratitude. Our life is never our own possession to be disposed of as we will. We receive life as a divine gift. We never use life as a commercial commodity. God is the author of all human life. God's presence in human fatherhood and motherhood means that just as God created Adam and Eve so he creates each person conceived in the womb. This is a matter of faith. We believe it on the word of God. God, not man, is the author of life. Therefore, life is always a gift; it is never a commodity.

The most horrendous crimes take place when life is treated as a commodity. When rulers see life as a commodity, a disposable human asset, the very security of the human race is undermined: conflicts which should be settled by reason lead to wars and destruction of life. Human life is sacrificed in the furtherance of some political ambition. So often the dignity of human life is sacrificed on the altar of economic greed: in the name of modernisation and economic efficiency hundreds of thousands of people are thrown out of work. Great profits are made by the few; hardship and unemployment have to be suffered by the many. When life is seen as a commodity economic efficiency will always take precedence over life. If a married couple see life as a commodity and not as a divine gift the avoidance of some perceived disadvantage to themselves or their family will always take precedence over the birth of a child: abortion, even if it is sought most reluctantly and after painful agonising, will ultimately be seen and justified in terms of economic or social or eugenic efficiency. When life is seen as a commodity and not as a divine gift the debility, the sufferings, the loneliness of old age will be terminated by induced death under the name of euthanasia. In fact, when life is seen as a commodity and not as a divine gift only 'high quality' life, in the sense of healthy, wealthy and successful, is regarded as worthwhile. The unborn and the old, the chronically handicapped and the terminally ill, are all at risk. Death and not life in abundance can become the objective of otherwise kind and loving carers.

So many good people are being misled by fallacious moral principles. If there is no objective truth about what is right and wrong people will ultimately judge the morality of everything by the impact it has on themselves. If it is helpful and convenient for themselves it will be declared good in itself; if it is unhelpful or inconvenient for themselves it will be declared bad in itself. Through this fallacious reasoning abortion or euthanasia or indeed any other behaviour that the Church has always considered wrong will be justified. Jesus' answer to the man who asked him, 'Master, what good deed must I do to possess eternal life' is God's word to each of us: 'Why do you ask me about what is good. There is one alone who is good. But if you wish to enter into life, keep the commandments' (Matt. 19:17). God's commandments are his life-giving word to us. As Scripture says, 'The law of the Lord is perfect, it gives life to the soul' (Ps. 19:7). To have within us the fullness of life which Jesus came to bring we must live in accordance with the life-giving word of God. This word is faithfully handed on to us by the Church which, as St Paul said, 'upholds the truth and keeps it safe' (1 Tim. 3:14). The mass media engage in a daily interpretation of the laws of life and the meaning of life and the behaviours which are acceptable in life. We have the Church as our teacher. As the Vatican Council said: 'The task of authentically interpreting the word of God, whether in its written form or in that of Tradition, has been entrusted only to those charged with the Church's living Magisterium, whose authority is exercised in the name of Jesus Christ.'[7] Christ alone is our teacher. The Church faithfully hands on Christ's teaching to us. We should never be surprised if our Christian teaching on life is unacceptable to the world around us. If we have to choose between what the papers say and what the Church says we have made that choice a long time ago. We made it when we said in the Creed: 'We believe in the one, holy, catholic and apostolic Church.' In the words of Cardinal Newman's well known hymn:

And I hold in veneration
for the love of him alone
Holy Church as his creation
and her teaching as his own.

The abundant life which Jesus came to give us begins with the gift of our physical life. That gift is sacred. But this gift takes on a whole new dimension when God fills the person whom he has created with his own divine life. Jesus spoke about this gift of divine life in terms of a rebirth:

I tell you solemnly,
unless a man is born through water and the Spirit,

137

he cannot enter the kingdom of God:
what is born of the flesh is flesh;
what is born of the Spirit is spirit. (John 3:6)

God creates not just our physical life; he also shares with us his own eternal life, making us his adopted sons and daughters. The very purpose and meaning of our life here on earth is to live gratefully in the full consciousness of who we are as children of God. St John encourages us to do that: 'Think of the love that the Father has lavished on us, by letting us be called God's children: and that is what we are' (1 John 3:1). We are invited to think on this love, to reflect on it, to ponder it in our hearts. When we do that we begin to develop a contemplative focus in our life. Our perspectives begin to change. Things which may have formerly loomed largely in our lives begin to take their proper place. Damian and Cathy Stayne, a young married couple, share with us how their perspectives on life changed when they opened themselves to the new and abundant life of Christ:

WE BOTH COME FROM CATHOLIC FAMILIES WITH DEEP FAITH, both sets of parents were active members of the church, locally and nationally. As young people we walked away from many of the values held by our parents and experienced as a result the confusion and pain that accompanies setting one's heart on things of this world and seeking fulfilment and meaning in temporal things. Having tasted the fruitlessness of pursuing life without God at the centre we both then had powerful adult conversion experiences, through involvement in the Catholic Charismatic Renewal. This gave us a new joy and a desire to live for God.

We first met each other at the South London Chaplaincy and got married five years later. We now lead a Catholic Charismatic Community called 'Cor Lumen Christi' (The Heart and Light of Christ) which has 45 members living various expressions of commitment on both a residential and non-residential basis. Our shared life involves evangelistic outreach, works of mercy, the simplification of our lifestyles, teaching, training, formation, the celebration of the sacraments, praise, worship, adoration and a deep life of prayer.

Living life closely with others who have also chosen to live for God before all else is extremely encouraging, challenging and rewarding. It empowers us to live a more radical gospel lifestyle than might otherwise be possible for us on our own. It dismantles our facades and false 'personas', demanding that the real person emerge and thus releases us to become more and more ourselves, which is actually a great relief. Deep communion is not possible between 'personas', only between real people. We have discovered that love can only be genuine when we are genuinely ourselves. We have found that a deeper love and freedom are now possible and life is far less superficial. The effect of this on our spiritual lives is to bring deeper reality and vulnerability into our relationship with God enabling us to more deeply 'receive the Holy Spirit' (John 20:22) and believe ourselves loved just as we are. This in turn brings greater peace and joy.

Life in the spirit in community is for us a full life which calls forth the gifts of its members. We experience a more healthy interdependence through our shared life and mission and each one has his or her role and part to play. We are highly motivated because we know that what we do has eternal consequences and that we can play a significant part in God's plan. The committed friendships and support we enjoy increase our effectiveness because we know we are all pulling together for a common purpose. While we recognise things are by no means perfect, we feel we do live a life that is very worthwhile, in which we are growing in God.

We now know that all we were searching for can be found in a life of deep communion with God. It is, we have discovered, a profound experience of this divine communion that is the longing of every human heart. We believe that the call to community is a strategy of the Holy Spirit to help people to enter into divine communion as a way of life and thus share in God's own experience of abundant life.

Damian and Cathy, through their conversion, got the grace to seek God and the kingdom of God before all other things. They began to live by the word of Jesus: 'Set your hearts on his kingdom first, and on his righteousness, and all these other things will be given you as well' (Matt. 6:33). Through their conversion they began to experience abundant life:

- fruitlessness of life without God at the centre
- a new joy and desire to live for God
- the gift of a community of committed men and women who are living for God
- a more radical gospel lifestyle
- the freedom and relief of dropping facades and being oneself
- a life of adoration, deep prayer and concern to reach out to others
- the emergence of the gifts of the Spirit in the members of the community
- committed friendship and support in community making their mission more effective
- all they were searching for can now be found in a life of deep communion with God
- the peace and joy that comes from knowing that their life is worthwhile and they are growing in God

The door to life in abundance is conversion. Through the grace of their conversion God has *hallowed his name* in Damian and Cathy and in the community of young men and women whom they lead.

Faith sharing

1. How does the belief that God dwells in your heart influence the way you see yourself and others?
2. Can you share a moment when this faith influenced the way you acted towards someone?
3. Have you any memories of when you totally ignored this truth in the way you related to others?

Scripture reading

The Second Vatican Council expressed this hope: 'So may it come that by reading and study of the sacred books "the Word of God may speed on and triumph" (2 Thess. 3:1) and the treasure of Revelation entrusted to the Church may more and more fill the hearts of all.'[8] We enrich our whole life by the daily reading of the word of God.

Sunday	Titus and Philemon
Monday	Hebrews 1—5
Tuesday	Hebrews 6—9
Wednesday	Hebrews 10—13
Thursday	James
Friday	1 Peter
Saturday	2 Peter

12

Finding God in all things

The psalmist sings: 'As a deer that yearns for running streams so my soul is yearning for you my God' (Ps. 42:1). The deepest yearning in the human heart, though we may not always recognise it, is for God. As St Augustine said: 'You have made us for yourself, O Lord, and our hearts will find no rest until they rest in you.' Our goal in life, the end and the purpose of our life, is union with God. The desire for this union keeps our hearts searching, restless, yearning. This desire will only be perfectly satisfied in heaven. But this desire is not just for that perfect union with God in heaven. God invites us, here and now, in this world, to live in union with him. He invites us to live in his presence; to listen to his voice; to speak to him; to serve him; and, most of all, to love him with our whole heart.

God wills us to live in union with him not just when we pray or when we go to church, but at all times and in all places. God is not just present when we pray. God is present in all things and in every situation. He is as truly present in the factory as he is in the church; he is as really present in our daily work as in our daily prayer. The world of work is not closed to the divine presence. God is absent from nothing. In fact, if God were absent we would have, literally, no thing. No thing could exist without God. Everything has its being from God. That is why St Paul says 'for all things give thanks to God, because this is what God expects you to do in Christ Jesus' (1 Thess. 5:17).

The Second Vatican Council sanctioned a whole new spirituality for the laity, a spirituality of the market place where God is truly present: 'By reason of their special vocation it belongs to the laity to seek the kingdom of God by engaging in temporal affairs and directing them according to God's will. They live in the world, that is, they are engaged in each and every work and business of the earth and in the ordinary circumstances of social and family life which, as it were constitute their very existence.'[1] From these situations and activities which constitute the very existence of the vast majority of the Church, namely the laity, God is not absent. At times, in the past, regrettably, the laity were given the impression that only those who 'left the world' for the priesthood or the religious life were on the 'high road' to heaven. In fact, this very insidious distinction was introduced into theology: religious were called to holiness by following the way of the evangelical counsels, namely the three vows of poverty, chastity and obedience, while the laity were called to salvation by following the way of the ten commandments. The Vatican Council officially ruled out such a spurious distinction. Pope John Paul has frequently reaffirmed the Council's teaching:

THE VOCATION OF THE LAY FAITHFUL TO HOLINESS IMPLIES that life according to the Spirit expresses itself in a particular way in their involvement in temporal affairs and in their participation in earthly activities. Once again the apostle admonishes us: 'whatever you do, in word or deed, do everything in the name of the Lord Jesus, giving thanks to God the Father through him' (Col. 3:17). Applying the apostle's words to the lay faithful, the Council categorically affirms: Neither family concerns nor other secular affairs should be excluded from their religious programme of life.[2]

Working in the midst of the world is not an obstacle to holiness of life because God is as present in the noise of the busy world as he is in the silence of a monastery. The God who is present to the monk in silence and prayer is equally present to the labourer in the fields or in the factory. The Vatican Council stated:

ONE OF THE GRAVEST ERRORS OF OUR TIME IS THE dichotomy between the faith which many profess and the practice of their daily lives ... Let there be no such pernicious opposition between professional and social activity on the one hand and religious life on the other. The Christian who shirks his temporal duties shirks his duties to his neighbour, neglects God himself, and endangers his eternal salvation.'3

The Church clearly teaches the good news that our life is not compartmentalised into the secular and the spiritual, into daily work and daily prayer, into action and contemplation. Our life is a unity. The more we integrate the secular and the spiritual the more unified our life becomes. The secret for this integration is finding God in all things. This requires training – training of heart and spirit.

Practical steps

Each of us has a contemplative capacity. We can look in wonder at beautiful things; we can be deeply moved by human joy or sorrow; we can be still and silent in the presence of loved ones. In each of these human emotions the deepest reality which we experience is the presence of God. But so often we have not woken up to that presence. The real difference between the contemplative and the non-contemplative is like the difference between a person who is enjoying his work and a person who is fast asleep. The person fast asleep is totally unaware of the world around him. He is in the land of slumber. Too often our spirit can be slumbering. Our bodies may be wide awake, full of all kinds of activities, full of human interests. But our spirits may be slumbering, unaware or just vaguely aware of the life that is happening within us and around us. Within us God is present, loving us, sustaining us and inviting us to a life of communion; outside us and all around us God is present in each event and in each situation. We need to waken up to his presence.

The poet and patriot Joseph Mary Plunkett, who was executed for his part in the Easter Rising in Dublin in 1916, was wide awake to God's presence in the world around him. His poem on this divine presence is well known:

I see his blood upon the rose
And in the stars the glory of his eyes,
His body gleams amid eternal snows
His tears fall from the skies.

I see his face in every flower
The thunder and the singing of the birds
are but his voice – and carven by his power
Rocks are his written words.

All pathways by his feet are worn,
His strong heart stirs the ever-beating sea,
His crown of thorns is twined with every thorn,
His cross is every tree.[4]

That is the contemplative spirit awake to the presence of God in all things. St Alphonsus Liguori, writing in the eighteenth century in Italy, gave this practical advice on this kind of prayer: 'When your eye rests on scenes in the country or along the shore, on flowers or fruits, and you are delighted by the sight and the scent of all, say, Behold, how many are the beautiful creatures that God has created for me in this world that I may love him; and what further enjoyments does he not keep prepared for me in paradise.'[5]

Sometimes we may find it easier to rejoice in God's presence when we behold some beautiful scene than to see Christ really present in another person. Yet we believe the words of Jesus: 'whatever you did to the least of my brethren you did to me.' Each person we encounter is a walking shrine of God's presence, a living tabernacle of Christ. Jesus has so identified himself with the human race that there is not a single human being who is not, in some way, the tabernacle of his presence. We may only see an enemy, or a drunk, or a beggar, or a lay about. The eye of faith sees Jesus. Faith is like borrowing the eyes of

Jesus to see what is really there. And what is really there in each person is the presence of Christ. To cultivate finding God in all things we should begin to find him where we believe he truly is, namely in the other.

If we wish to grow in this spirituality of finding God in all things we must discipline our minds and hearts to enable our spirit to remain awake. This is the importance of morning prayer – first thing in the morning. As we wake up to the new day we should wake up our spirit to the presence of God. We should begin immediately to praise God. You may say that morning is not your best time. But you do not have to make eloquent speeches to God. All you have to do is to acknowledge his presence with you, thank him for the new day, and offer him all your thoughts words and actions of the day. It makes no difference if you are still sleepy. A sleepy morning offering will have the same effect on your spirit as a chirpy one!

The simple prayer of 'grace before meals' can teach us a great deal about how to find God in all things. You have just prepared a meal. You sit down to enjoy it with your family or by yourself. You say: 'Bless us, O Lord, and these thy gifts which we are about to receive from your bounty through Christ the Lord.' You have done the shopping; you have prepared the food; you have cooked the meal. Yet, in this prayer we acknowledge that it is all from God. God was in your shopping and in your preparation; he was in your cooking and in your enjoying. That 'grace before meals' is an appropriate prayer before you begin any work. As I begin to type this page I can say: 'Bless us, O Lord, and these thy gifts.' And as I think about the chapter which I have just finished I can say: 'We give thee thanks, O almighty God for all thy benefits.' God is present in all things. Prayer is like wakening up to his presence. By staying awake in his presence we will be able to find him in all things.

God in troubled times

What about the hard times and the bad times? Should we find God in those times too? After a healing service in which I had been leading a parish community in prayers of thanksgiving to God for his holy and hidden presence in all the trouble and tragedies of life, a family of six waited for me – the two parents, two sons and two daughters. They were all crying. I thought I might have upset them by something I said. 'O no', the mother said 'our sixteen-year-old daughter was raped and murdered a year ago today and now we know that she wasn't all alone. Christ was with her.' Their greatest pain came from the thought of their dear daughter all alone as her assassin brutalised and killed her. As they began to acknowledge the presence of God they got the grace to see that despite the awful crime, despite their terrible loss, God was present. They were able to surrender their horror at her being all alone to God. They did not ask 'why did God not stop the murderer?' That can be such a stumbling block. We believe that God is all loving and all powerful. Then why does he not stop wars, save the innocent, prevent disasters like earthquakes? Our Blessed Lady could have asked that at the foot of the cross. Christ's enemies did: 'As for the leaders of the people, they jeered at him. "He saved others, let him save himself if he is the Christ of God, the Chosen One" ' (Luke 23:35).

St Paul faced this agonising question: where is God when evil things happen? He wrote:

WITH GOD ON OUR SIDE WHO CAN BE AGAINST US? SINCE God did not spare his own Son, but gave him up to benefit us all, we may be certain, after such a gift, that he will not refuse us anything he can give. Could anyone accuse those that God has chosen? When God acquits, could anyone condemn? Could Christ Jesus? No! He not only died for us – he rose from the dead, and there at God's right hand he stands and pleads for us.

Nothing therefore can come between us and the love of Christ, even if we are troubled and worried, or being persecuted, or lacking food and clothes, or being threatened or even attacked. As Scripture promised: for your sake we are being massacred daily, and reckoned as sheep for the slaughter. These are the trials through which we triumph, by the power of him who loves us.

For I am certain of this: neither death nor life, no angel, no prince, nothing that exists, nothing still to come, not any power, or height or depth, nor any created thing, can ever come between us and the love of God made visible in Christ Jesus our Lord. (Rom. 8:31–39)

To the person without faith Paul's answer is no answer; to the person with living faith no further answer is needed. I believe that grieving family had living faith. If the all-powerful Father did not stop his Son from being nailed to the cross they were not going to ask him why he did not stop their daughter being murdered.

St Alphonsus Liguori, a man who knew great trouble in his own life, wrote:

WHEN, THEREFORE, YOU ARE AFFLICTED WITH A SICKNESS, temptation, persecution, or other trouble, go at once and ask him that his hand may help you. It is enough for you to present your affliction to him: to come in and say 'Look, O Lord, upon my distress' (Lam. 1:20) he will not fail to comfort you, or at least to give you strength to suffer that grief with patience; and it will turn out a greater good to you than if you were already freed from it. Tell him all the thoughts of fear or of sadness that torment you and say to him 'My God in you are all my hopes; I offer you this affliction and resign myself to your will; but do you take pity on me – either deliver me out of it, or give me the strength to bear it.'[6]

St Alphonsus knew from his own experience that in time of trouble fine theories are of little avail. We need living faith which enables us to reach out to God who is present in the midst of the trouble or grief and ask for help. At such times we can better understand the meaning of Jesus' words: 'unless you become like little children you will not enter the kingdom of God.' The little child cries out to its mother or father in time of need. Trouble or grief by itself is bad enough; trouble or grief from which we exclude God by not crying out to him for help, like a little child, can be unbearable. That is why St Paul encouraged the early Christians 'not to grieve about the dead, like the other people who have no hope' (1 Thess. 4:13). Paul is saying grieve by all means, but grieve with hope in the resurrection. The immediate pain of loss will be the same, but the assurance in faith that the loved one is with God will bring comfort and consolation in due course.

Sr Phyllis Hughes shares with us how she has been led to find God in all things:

IN THE COURSE OF A TELEPHONE CONVERSATION ONE evening, Jim asked me the following question: How do you find God in all things? My immediate response to the question 'how do you find God in all things?' is this: I find God in the beauty and goodness of the people who are in my life, in the freshness and newness of nature especially at the moment when Spring with all its wonderment and new life surrounds us.

God is at the centre of my being, of my reason for living and he continually surrounds me in my everyday life, in people and situations I encounter.

My answer to the question was immediate and sincere, but while reflecting on this question since that evening, I realise that, yes, I do find God in the vastness of the sea, the wonder in a child's eyes, in the love of my family, friends and members of my community.

I find God in the stillness of my prayer. Christ comes alive in the listening to and the praying of the Gospels, through the celebration, the sharing and the living out of the Eucharist and reconciliation. I am aware of my need of the Spirit and the strength which she gives. God is very close too when I listen to others and pray with them in their struggles and joys. The trust given to me and the trust that I give to others is for me a true discovery of God in my life and in all life.

Being an optimist by nature, it has always been relatively easy for me to find God in beauty, stillness, love and wonder. My journey through the latter years of my life has really brought me to find God in pain and suffering.

I have had to struggle to find him in the pain and questioning of the sudden death of my younger brother. There has been a struggle too because of events and situations surrounding my apostolic mission in life. Pain, confusion and even questioning God himself have brought me to a deeper and perhaps a more real relationship with him.

Pain and suffering were no strangers to me in the earlier years of my life, but somehow during the stage of mid-life I have been led to discover and embrace God through the reality of the Paschal Mystery (death and resurrection of Jesus), in my own brokenness and fragility, in my dying and my rising.

In the past few years of my life I have struggled with poor health. Optimists usually enjoy life to the full, and I am no exception! To experience physical weakness, to arrive at acknowledging my dependency on others, having to admit to being unreliable have brought me to an awareness of my complete and utter dependence on God.

It has been and continues to be a painful journey but I am deeply convinced of the personal love that God has for me and of my love for him. Yes, I know that God is in the joys and dreams, the sorrows and brokenness of my life. I can identify more and more with the words of St Paul: 'When I am weak, then I am strong.'

Sr Phyllis clearly identifies her own experience of life as the major source of God's experiential presence. We can highlight where she finds God:

- in beauty and goodness

- at the centre of my being
- in listening to and praying the Gospels
- in listening to others
- in pain, confusion and questioning
- in brokeness and fragility
- in the experience of physical weakness and dependency

As the Vatican Council said: 'The joy and hope, the grief and anguish of the men of our time, especially of those who are poor or afflicted in any way, are the joy and hope, the grief and anguish of the followers of Christ as well.'[7] God does not anaesthetise us against pain; he is not a panacea for all our woes. Sr Phyllis shares, from her own personal experience, the view of her fellow Scot, philosopher John Macmurray who said: 'The maxim of illusory religion runs: "Fear not; trust in God and he will see that none of the things you fear will happen to you;" that of real religion, on the contrary, is: "Fear not; the things that you are afraid of are quite likely to happen to you, but they are nothing to be afraid of." '[8] God is our loving Father, present with us in all our struggles, sustaining, encouraging and enabling us to face each new day, despite its troubles, with confidence. He never said that we would not have troubles in this world. But he promised that he would be with us in all of them. Indeed, as St Paul discovered, because God helps us in our troubles we are able to help others in their troubles: 'Blessed be the God and Father of our Lord Jesus Christ, a gentle Father and the God of all consolation, who comforts us in all our sorrows, so that we can offer others, in their sorrows, the consolation that we have received from God ourselves' (2 Cor. 1:3–6). Paul is saying that because he found God's help in his troubles he can now use that help to help others in their trouble.

Contemplating the cross of Christ is the best preparation of mind and heart for finding God in all things. God was so present in the crucifixion that it was God himself who died on the cross. Pain, suffering, failure and sickness, even death itself are not closed to the redeeming presence of God. God's redeeming presence in Jesus on the cross and in the tomb was the guarantee of the transformation of the resurrection. In the same way God's redeeming presence in all the circumstances of our lives, good or bad, guarantees our final victory in our resurrection from the dead.

Because God is truly present in each situation we should make it our special concern to acknowledge his divine presence. We can celebrate *the sacrament of the present moment* because it is in the present moment that God, Father, Son and Holy Spirit, is present to us. We should use very simple, ordinary means for this celebration of the sacrament of the present moment. St Alphonsus, my founder, kept a clock on his table which chimed every fifteen minutes. Whenever the clock chimed Alphonsus opened himself more consciously to the presence of God and lived that moment more intensely aware that God was with him. His example became a great help to me one year. I was a student in our international house in Rome. I lived on the third corridor. Just outside my door there was a phone. It rang very frequently. I was expected to answer it and then find the student who was being asked for. For the first day or two I did not mind doing this service. But I quickly began to resent it. I resented being disturbed at my studies or at my rest. My resentment was turning into anger and an unwillingness to answer the phone. Then I got the grace to remember St Alphonsus' clock. The phone could be my 'spiritual alarm clock'. I said to myself each time that wretched phone rings I will take it as a call from God to become aware of his presence. From then on the ring of the phone woke up my slumbering spirit. As I walked to answer the phone I was able to become aware of God's presence with me. In fact, that phone became the occasion of my best prayer during that year. Every time it rang outside my door I was able to 'raise my mind and heart to God'. For me God was on the line.

If we practise the presence of God, if we celebrate the sacrament of the present moment, in the ordinary situations of our daily life we will be prepared to find God in all things. And it is in the present moment that God wishes to hallow his name in our lives. When we pray 'hallowed be thy name' we are praying for the grace to find God in all things and to celebrate the sacrament of the present moment. We pray with confidence *'hallowed be thy name'*.

Faith sharing

1. Can you share one circumstance of the past week in which you found God present?
2. Do you recall how you reacted to situations in which you did not find God present?
3. How do you propose to practise the presence of God in your daily life?

Scripture reading

'The Church has always venerated the divine Scriptures as she venerated the Body of the Lord, in so far as she never ceases, particularly in the sacred liturgy, to partake of the Word of God and the Body of Christ . . . In the sacred books the Father who is in heaven comes lovingly to meet his children, and talks with them.'[9] As you meet God the Father in your reading of the Scriptures this week ask him for the grace of veneration for the Scriptures and as you complete the New Testament begin your prayerful reading of the gospels once again.

Sunday	1 John 1—2
Monday	1 John 3—4
Tuesday	2 John, 3 John, Jude
Wednesday	Revelation 1—3
Thursday	Revelation 4—10
Friday	Revelation 11—17
Saturday	Revelation 18—22

Notes

Introduction

1 John Paul II, *Mission of the Redeemer* (1991), 49.
2 ibid. 42.
3 ibid. 42.
4 ibid. 49.
5 ibid. 91.

1 Hallowed be thy name

1 Gerhard Lohfink, *Jesus and Community* (London, SPCK, 1985), p. 15.
2 Cited by *Catechism of the Catholic Church* (London, Geoffrey Chapman, 1994), p. 598, para. 2814.
3 ibid., p. 597, para. 2813.
4 ibid., p. 598, para. 2814.
5 ibid., p. 598, para. 2809.
6 cf. R. Brown et al. (eds.), *Jerome Biblical Commentary* (London, Geoffrey Chapman, 1970), vol. 2, p. 144, para. 104.
7 John Paul II, *Crossing the Threshold of Hope* (London, Jonathan Cape, 1994), p. 58.
8 John Paul II, *Evangelium Vitae* (1994), 99.
9 Quoted by Leanne Payne, *Restoring the Christian Soul through Healing Prayer* (Eastbourne, Kingsway, 1992), p. 31.
10 John Paul II, *Redemptor Hominis* (1979), 10.
11 Decree on Divine Revelation, *Dei Verbum*, 25.

2 Living by the word of God

1 Quoted by Michael Crosby, *Thy Will Be Done* (New York, 1977), p. 38.
2 *Catechism of the Catholic Church* (London, Geoffrey Chapman, 1994), p. 83, para. 387.
3 *New Rite of Penance*, 7.
4 C. S. Lewis, *Fern-Seed and Elephants* (Glasgow, Fount, 1975), p. 40.
5 Nelson Mandela, *Long Walk to Freedom* (London, Little, Brown, 1994), p. 376.
6 ibid. p. 304.
7 *Dei Verbum*, 21.

3 Getting to know the word of God

1 *Osservatore Romano* (English edn), 19 May 1986.
2 *Dei Verbum*, 13.
3 ibid. 11.
4 Gerald O'Collins, *Priests and People*, April, 1995, p. 150.
5 *Dei Verbum*, 11.
6 *Catechism of the Catholic Church* (London, Geoffrey Chapman, 1994), p. 29, para. 102.
7 *Dei Verbum*, 21.
8 Introduction to the Roman Missal, 9.
9 Constitution on the Liturgy, *Sacrosanctum Concilium*, 24.
10 *Dei Verbum*, 21.
11 ibid.
12 *Dei Verbum*, 21.

4 The word in prayer

1 *Dei Verbum*, 21.
2 ibid. 25.
3 Office of Readings, 23 December.
4 *Veritatis Splendor* (1994), 19.

5 *Dei Verbum*, 10.
6 Tom Smail, *The Giving Gift* (London, Darton, Longman and Todd, 1994), p. 208.
7 New Rite of Penance, 6.
8 M. Maddocks, *The Christian Healing Ministry* (London, SPCK, 1985), p. 12.
9 Quoted by R. Cantalamessa, *Life in the Lordship of Christ* (London, Darton, Longman and Todd, 1992), p. 48.
10 *Dei Verbum*, 21.

5 Living by the word of promise

1 Viktor Frankl, *The Unheard Cry for Meaning* (New York, Simon and Schuster, 1978), p. 34.
2 Nelson Mandela, *Long Road to Freedom* (London, Little, Brown, 1994), p. 376.
3 Decree on Non-Christian Religions, *Nostra Aetate*, para. 4.
4 I. De La Potterie and S. Lyonnet, *The Christian Lives by the Spirit* (New York, 1970), p. 158.
5 Quoted by R. Cantalamessa, *Life in the Lordship of Jesus*, p. 151.
6 Killian McDonald and George Montague, *Christian Initiation and Baptism in the Spirit* (Collegeville, MN, 1991), p. 21.

6 Abba, Father

1 Kinnoull refers to the Redemptorist Mission and Renewal Centre in Scotland where priests and religious, from all over the world, go for renewal courses and retreat.
2 *Catechism of the Catholic Church* (London, Geoffrey Chapman, 1994), p. 14, para. 27.
3 ibid. para. 28.
4 ibid. p. 50, para. 203.
5 ibid. p. 57, para. 239.
6 Office of Readings, Monday 1st week of Lent.
7 ibid., Tuesday, week 10.

7 Jesus Christ is Lord

1 Yves Congar, *I Believe in the Holy Spirit* (London, Geoffrey Chapman, 1987), vol. 1, p. 23.
2 ibid. p. 36.
3 St Irenaeus, quoted in *Catechism of the Catholic Church* (London, Geoffrey Chapman, 1994), p. 96, para. 432.
4 R. Cantalamessa, *The Holy Spirit in the Life of Jesus* (Collegeville, MN, 1994), p. 6.
5 ibid. p. 7.
6 *Catechism*, p. 98, para 438.
7 Encyclical on the Holy Spirit (1986), 19.
8 Cantalamessa, *Holy Spirit*, p. 5.
9 Decree on Priests, *Presbyterorum Ordinis*, 1.
10 Romano Guardini, *The Lord* (London, Longman Green, 1954), p. 446.
11 *Catechism*, p. 152, para. 664.
12 *Dei Verbum*, 11.

8 Jesus the Lord sends us the Holy Spirit

1 Tom Smail, *The Giving Gift*, p. 105.
2 Constitution on the Church, *Lumen Gentium*, 7.
3 ibid. 40.
4 Decree on Ecumenism, *Unitatis Redintegratio*, 2.
5 *Lumen Gentium*, 9.
6 Smail, p. 173.
7 ibid. p. 209 (quoting André Louf).
8 ibid. p. 167.
9 Aquinas, *Commentary on Hebrews*, Cap. 8, lect. 2.
10 Aquinas, *Commentary on 2 Corinthians*, Cap. 3, lect. 2.
11 Aquinas, *Summa Theologiae*, 1a 2ae, Q. 106, art. 1.
12 I. De La Potterie and S. Lyonnet, *The Christian Lives by the Spirit* (New York, 1970), p. 158.
13 Encyclical on the Holy Spirit (1986), 31.
14 *Dei Verbum*, 31.

9 The gifts of the Holy Spirit

1 *Presbyterorum Ordinis*, 13.
2 *Tertio Millennio Adveniente*, 1994.
3 Killian McDonald, *The Holy Spirit and Power* (New York, Doubleday & Co Inc., 1975), p. 123.
4 *Lumen Gentium*, 12.
5 F. Sullivan, *Charisms and Charismatic Renewal* (Ann Arbor, Servant, 1982), p. 13.
6 *Redemptor Hominis*, 8.
7 *Dei Verbum*, 9.

10 'We will come to him and make our home with him'

1 Constitution on the Church in the Modern World, *Gaudium et Spes*, 2.
2 St Augustine, *Confessions*, bk 10, ch. 27.
3 *Dei Verbum*, 17.

11 Life in abundance

1 *Evangelium Vitae*, 7.
2 *Catechism of the Catholic Church*, p. 476, para. 2259.
3 *Evangelium Vitae*, 80.
4 ibid.
5 ibid.
6 ibid.
7 *Dei Verbum*, 10.
8 *Dei Verbum*, 26.

12 Finding God in all things

1 *Lumen Gentium*, 31.
2 Apostolic Exhortation on the Vocation of the Laity, (1988), 17.

3 *Gaudium et Spes*, 43.
4 Desmond Ryan (ed.), *The 1916 Poets* (Dublin, Allen Figgis, 1963), p. 192.
5 Carl Hoergerl, *Heart call to Heart: An Alphonsian Anthology* (Rome, 1981), p. 219.
6 ibid., p. 206.
7 *Gaudium et Spes*, 1.
8 Quoted by William A. Barry, *Paying Attention to God* (Notre Dame, 1990), p. 29.
9 *Dei Verbum*, 21.